God's Plan for Giving

God's Plan for Giving

by
John MacArthur, Jr.

MOODY PRESS
CHICAGO

Library of Congress Cataloging-In-Publication Data

MacArthur, John F.
    God's plan for giving.

    (John MacArthur's Bible studies)
    1. Christian giving.   2. Christian giving — Biblical
teaching.   3. Money — Biblical teaching.   4. Bible —
Criticism, interpretation, etc.   I. Title.   II. Series:
MacArthur, John F.   Bible studies.
    BV772.M255   1985   248'.6   85-21652
    ISBN 0-8024-5107-1 (pbk.)

9 10 11 12 Printing/EP/Year 95 94 93 92 91

Printed in the United States of America

Contents

These Bible studies are taken from messages delivered by Pastor-Teacher John MacArthur, Jr., at Grace Community Church in Panorama City, California. The recorded messages themselves may be purchased as a series or individually. Please request the current price list by writing to:

WORD OF GRACE COMMUNICATIONS
P.O. Box 4000
Panorama City, CA 91412

Or call the following toll-free number:
1-800-55-GRACE

1

The Christian and His Finances

Outline

Introduction

Lesson
I. The Right to Possess Money
   A. God Owns All Money
      1. Haggai 2:8
      2. Deuteronomy 8:18*a*
      3. 1 Corinthians 4:7*b*
   B. God Gives Men the Power to Gain Money
   C. God Doesn't Condemn Money
   D. God Provides Principles for Gaining Wealth
      1. Work
         a) Proverbs 14:23
         b) 2 Thessalonians 3:10–11
         c) Proverbs 6:6–8
         d) Proverbs 20:4
         e) 1 Timothy 5:8
      2. Save
      3. Plan
         a) Proverbs 27:23–24*a*
         b) Proverbs 24:3–4
   E. God Wants Us to Be Debt Free
      1. Romans 13:8*a*
      2. Proverbs 22:7*b*
      3. 1 Corinthians 7:23
   F. God Doesn't Want Us to Be a Loan Company

II. The Way to Regard Money
   A. The Cautions of Loving Money
      1. The desire is never satisfied
      2. The desire leads to more evil
      3. The desire lacks contentment
      4. The desire separates man from God

7

B. The Consequences of Loving Money
1. Forget God
2. Stop trusting God
   a) Job 31:24–25, 28b
   b) Proverbs 11:28
   c) 1 Timothy 6:17–18
3. Be deceived
4. Compromise biblical instruction
5. Rest on unstable foundations
6. Be ungrateful
7. Be proud
   a) Proverbs 28:11a
   b) Jeremiah 12:2
8. Rob God
9. Rob others

III. The Way to Give Money
A. Giving Should Be in Response to Need
B. Giving Should Be in Response to God's Command
C. Giving Should Be Sacrificial
D. Giving Should Be Secret and Humble
E. Giving Is the Key to Spiritual Fruit

Introduction

Money, in a sense, is life, because we spend all our lives getting it for the purpose of staying alive. Now money itself is amoral; it's not good, and it's not bad. But depending on how it is used, it becomes either good or bad. So money can cause either righteous or unrighteous ramifications in our lives. Thus, our concept of money becomes very important. For this study we will examine three categories: the right to possess money, the way to regard money, and the way to give money.

Lesson

I. THE RIGHT TO POSSESS MONEY

There are some people in the world who call themselves Christians and say it is wrong for a Christian to have any money. They advocate a kind of Christian communism and base it on Acts 2:44–45, which says they "had all things common." Therefore, they say that all Christians should get into some kind of community where they give everything to a central source. That source then doles out everything on an equal basis according to need. Consequently, the Christian has no right to possess money. Well, let's see what the Bible teaches.

We must understand that:

A. God Owns All Money

1. Haggai 2:8—"The silver is mine, and the gold is mine, saith the Lord of hosts." God was referring to all the nations, and He said all their silver and gold really belonged to Him.

2. Deuteronomy 8:18a—"But thou shalt remember the Lord thy God; for it is he who giveth thee power to get wealth." God is the One to grant men the power to get wealth because it belongs to Him.

3. 1 Corinthians 4:7b—"And what hast thou that thou didst not receive?" Now you can only give to somebody else what belongs to you. So if God gives you money, then it was His to begin with.

B. God Gives Men the Power to Gain Money

The Bible does not assume that it's wrong to have money, but rather that God allows men to make money. Money is actually one of God's gifts, but man has a way of twisting and perverting all of God's gifts, including money. First Timothy 6:17c says that God "giveth us richly all things to enjoy." God is not some browbeating ogre who wants everybody in pain and misery. He gives us much to enjoy. So, God, the possessor of all moneys, is willing to grant some to us.

C. God Doesn't Condemn Money

In Acts 2:45 it says of the early church is Jerusalem: "And [they] sold their possessions and goods, and parted them to all men, as every man had need." As I mentioned before, some people take this to be a sort of Christian communism, but that's because they don't understand the Greek tense. The verbs "sold" and "parted" are both in the imperfect tense, which means it was a continuous action. It should read this way: "And were selling their possessions and goods, and were parting them to all men, as every man had need." It simply means that all the believers were selling their goods and giving money to those who had need as the needs arose. It was a picture of self-sacrifice for the need of another, not of pooling everything. Nowhere does the Bible advocate that all moneys be put into a common pot to be doled out by some hierarchy.

The same thing appears in Acts 4:34–35: "Neither was there any among them that lacked; for as many as were possessors of lands or houses sold them, and brought the prices of the things that were sold, and laid them down at the apostles' feet; and distribution was made unto every man according as he had need.'' So, when a person had a need, somebody was willing to sell something, get the money, and go meet that man's need. That's all it was advocating.

So the Bible does not forbid money belonging to men. In fact, the Bible says all money is God's, and God actually desires men to gain it. God wants to bless men with a certain amount of wealth.

D. God Provides Principles for Gaining Wealth

Now when I use the term *wealth*, I mean *something* as opposed to *nothing*. I'm not talking about being rich, I'm just talking about the term wealth as it is used biblically. There are some biblical principles that tell us how a man might gain a measure of wealth.

1. Work

    a) Proverbs 14:23—"In all labor there is profit, but mere talk leads only to poverty" (NASB*). God has designed that labor brings a measure of wealth and prosperity. He has given us work in order that we might gain wealth.

    b) 2 Thessalonians 3:10–11—"For even when we were with you, this we commanded you, that if any would not work, neither should he eat. For we hear that there are some who walk among you disorderly, working not at all but are busybodies." Work is a practical principle.

    c) Proverbs 6:6–8—"Go to the ant, thou sluggard; consider her ways, and be wise, which, having no guide, overseer, or ruler, provideth her food in the summer, and gathereth her food in the harvest." Lazy people should check out the ant, who doesn't have any employer yet does the job.

    d) Proverbs 20:4—"The sluggard will not plow by reason of the cold; therefore shall he beg in harvest, and have nothing."

    e) 1 Timothy 5:8—"But if any provide not for his own, and specially for those of his own house, he hath denied the faith, and is worse than an infidel."

    Work is designed by God to bring you money, because God knows that you have to have it to exist.

2. Save

    Proverbs 21:20 states, "There is precious treasure and oil in the dwelling of the wise, but a foolish man swallows it up"

New American Standard Bible.

(NASB). Do you know what a wise man does? He sets aside some of his treasure and some of his oil for the unexpected. Do you know what the fool does? He swallows it all up. *The Living Bible* has a good translation of this verse: "The wise man saves for the future, but the foolish man spends whatever he gets." One good way to save is to always operate on a margin. If you don't, then you may be presuming on the grace of God, hoping that He'll meet your need. For instance, instead of buying a nice little transportation car, you go out and buy a "Belch-Fire Eight." Then you say, "Well, God will provide." Be careful that you don't presume on God and extend yourself to the place where there's no margin left. Then when a crisis comes, you've got to presume on God to provide for your foolishness. David said, "Keep back thy servant also from presumptuous sins" (Ps. 19:13a). Those kinds of sins are illustrated in Matthew 4:5–7: "Then the devil taketh him up into the holy city, and setteth him on a pinnacle of the temple, and saith unto him, If thou be the Son of God, cast thyself down; for it is written, He shall give his angels charge concerning thee, and in their hands they shall bear thee up. . . . Jesus said unto him, It is written again, Thou shalt not put the Lord, thy God, to the test." Don't put yourself in a situation that you've gotten into by your foolishness, and then demand that God extract you. That's presumption, and it's sin.

Mr. and Mrs. Average American Couple

Imagine a married couple that doesn't operate on a margin. As so many couples do, they follow the great American way, which is to buy the things you don't need, with the money you don't have, from the people you don't even like. They get themselves in a situation where they are overextended, and they have more obligations than they do income. Along the way, they've taken under their wing the support of their local church and some friends who have gone to the mission field. What happens? Well, pretty soon they find that they can't meet those missionaries' needs, and they can't give to their local ministry. Then maybe they get to the place where they face bankruptcy, the loss of the car, the loss of the house, the loss of the job, and the loss of their testimony. Now they are limited as to what they can do for God because they have to pay for their foolishness with every dime they get. If God ever came to them and called them away to some mission field, they couldn't go.

God wants every Christian to have money. In fact, He wants you to have more money than you need. God's principle in Scripture is spend some—and save.

3. Plan

For some people, their budget is based on this principle: "Oh well, it will all work out in the end." Actually, planning means a budget, which may or may not be very sophisticated. But it means that there should be a priority list, and the keeping of records, so you know where you are. After all, whose money are you handling? It's God's money. You may say, "But I gave Him His tenth." Now wait a minute. I believe tithing is totally irrelevant. How much is God's? All of it is His. In fact, if I were working for a corporation, and I handled their money like I handle God's money, they'd have me in prison for misuse of funds. Thank the Lord for grace. Nevertheless, it's all His money.

But where do I get this idea about keeping records? Well, let's look at a couple of Scripture verses:

a) Proverbs 27:23–24a—"Know well the condition of your flocks, and pay attention to your herds; for riches are not forever" (NASB). That's good advice. You ought to know how many flocks you have, and you ought to know what condition they're in, because your money is not going to last forever. You need to know where you are financially at all times.

b) Proverbs 24:3–4—"Any enterprise is built by wise planning, becomes strong through common sense, and profits wonderfully by keeping abreast of the facts." That's from *The Living Bible*, which normally I don't prefer, but in this case it has an accurate paraphrase. Any successful venture is one where you keep abreast of the facts.

Now, let's look briefly at a key concept:

E. God Wants Us Debt Free

1. Romans 13:8a—"Owe no man anything, but to love one another." The only debt we ought to have is love. We should just keep paying love. But do you know what happens when you owe somebody something? Now I'm not talking about when you're faithfully making your house payment. I'm talking about when you're overdue, and when you're overextended.

2. Proverbs 22:7b—"The borrower is servant to the lender." You become the slave of that man to whom you owe something, and when you become the slave to some financial situation, you've violated a biblical principle.

3. 1 Corinthians 7:23—"Ye are bought with a price; be not yet the servants of men." A Christian should always be free enough to respond to whatever God wants him to do at any moment.

F. God Doesn't Want Us to Be a Loan Company

Since God doesn't want us to become a loan company, what do we do if a person comes up and says that he needs money to buy something? First of all, determine if it's a necessity. If it's not a necessity, don't loan it to him. But if he says that it is a necessity, don't loan it to him either—give it to him. First John 3:17 says, "But whosoever hath this world's good, and seeth his brother have need, and shutteth up his compassions from him, how dwelleth the love of God in him?" If he needs it, give it to him.

Another verse that speaks regarding loaning money is Proverbs 17:18: "It is poor judgment to countersign another's note, to become responsible for his debts" (TLB*). If he fails to pay, then you're held responsible.

But Why Am I Always Short of Money?

When you don't have enough money, ask yourself these questions:

1. Do I really need more?

2. Is God testing my faith?

3. Did I already misuse what He gave me?

4. Have I violated biblical principles?

Now you may say, "What biblical principles?" Well, let's take a look at a few of them.

a) Stinginess—Proverbs 11:24 says, "There is one who scatters, yet increases all the more, and there is one who withholds what is justly due, but it results only in want" (NASB).

b) Hastiness—Some of us, when we see something that we want, get all excited, and we've got to have it and we've got to have it now. But Proverbs 21:5b says, "But everyone who is hasty comes surely to poverty" (NASB). We need to be patient. Philippians 4:19a says, "But my God shall supply all your need."

c) Stubbornness—This is the attitude that says that you're going to do whatever you want with your money. However, Proverbs 13:18a says, "Poverty and shame will come to him who neglects discipline" (NASB).

*The Living Bible.

d) Laziness—Maybe you don't have any money because you are lazy. Proverbs 20:13 states, "Do not love sleep, lest you become poor; open your eyes, and you will be satisfied with food" (NASB). Proverbs 23:21*b* says, "Drowsiness will clothe a man with rags" (NASB).

e) Indulgence—Proverbs 23:21*a* says, "For the heavy drinker and the glutton will come to poverty" (NASB).

f) Craftiness—Proverbs 28:19 tells us, "He who tills his land will have plenty of food, but he who follows empty pursuits will have poverty in plenty" (NASB). Hard-working people do well, but those who pull shady deals will be broken.

If you don't have enough money, you may have violated one of these principles.

God wants you to have money. He wants you to have enough to live on so that all your needs are met. And He wants you to have a margin so that you'll be available to respond to the leading of the Holy Spirit. If you don't have enough, then you need to backtrack and find out what's wrong, or determine if God is bringing you through a time of tightness to test your faith.

II. THE WAY TO REGARD MONEY

Money can be a great blessing, but the key to it is what you think of it. Now you often hear people say, "Well, if I had a million dollars I'd give a lot to the Lord." No, they wouldn't. The question is not what you would do with a million; the question is, What are you doing with the ten in your pocket?

Now let's look at some thoughts regarding the love of money.

A. The Cautions of Loving Money

1. The desire is never satisfied

Ecclesiastes 5:10*a*, 11 says, "He who loves money will not be satisfied with money. . . . When good things increase, those who consume them increase. So what is the advantage to their owners except to look on?" (NASB). *The Living Bible* says it is this way: "The more you have, the more you spend, right up to the limits of your income, so what is the advantage of wealth — except perhaps to watch it as it runs through your fingers!" (Eccles. 5:11). No, it is not a question of having more and doing more with it—it is just a question of what you're doing with what you have. Actually, rich people have more problems. Jesus said in Mark 10:23*b*: "With what difficulty shall they that have riches enter into the kingdom of God!"

2. The desire leads to more evil

The apostle Paul said in 1 Timothy 6:10*a*, "For the love of money is the root of all evil." But notice that it doesn't say money is the root of all evil. It says "the *love* of money is the root of all evil." We can have a lot of it and not love it, or we can have none of it and love it. It's the love of money, not money. Money is amoral.

It is a question of attitude. What is your attitude toward money? Money can be such a powerful force in our lives because we deal with it all the time. Do you realize that, in normal circumstances, you are never without money? It's always a part of your life. That's why it's so important that you have the right attitude toward it.

3. The desire lacks contentment

First Timothy 6 also states, "But godliness with contentment is great gain; for we brought nothing into this world, and it is certain we can carry nothing out" (vv. 6–7). Godliness and contentment go together. Hebrews 13:5*b* adds, "And be content with such things as ye have."

If a person loves money, you'll find that it will bring all kinds of problems. In 1 Timothy 6:9*a* it says, "But they that will be rich . . ." Now that's tantamount to loving money. I've even heard people say, "Well, I'm going to make a million so I can give it to the Lord." Don't make a million for the Lord—the Lord's not poor. Please don't cloak your own desire to be a rich man in that kind of a guise. "But seek ye first the kingdom of God, and his righteousness" (Matt. 6:33*a*), then, let the Lord worry about whether or not He gives you a million dollars. Now getting back to 1 Timothy 6:9: "But they that will be rich fall into temptation and a snare, and into many foolish and hurtful lusts, which drown men in destruction and perdition." "Perdition" means "loss." When a person loves money, he is useless to God.

4. The desire separates man from God

Jesus summed it up this way, "Ye cannot serve God and money" (Matt. 6:24*d*). For money, Achan brought defeat on Israel's army and death to himself and his family (Josh. 7). For money, Balaam sinned against light and tried to curse the living God (Num. 22:1–22; cf. 31:8,16). For money, Delilah betrayed Samson (Judg. 16:4–31). For money, Ananias and Sapphira became the first hypocrites in the church, and God executed them as a testimony against their misuse of money

15

and their deceit (Acts 5:1–11). For money, Judas sold Jesus (Matt. 26:14–16). Not very good company for money lovers.

B. The Consequences of Loving Money

What does loving money lead to? Let's look at some of the things that can happen. Loving money leads people to:

1. Forget God

Most of the book of Proverbs was written by Solomon, except for chapter 30, which was written by a man named Agur. Now Agur may have watched Solomon, and Solomon was rich beyond belief. But he became trapped in his riches, and he wanted more and more. So he kept marrying foreign wives to bring in more treasure. Solomon brought Israel into idolatry and it ruined his life. Agur may have had Solomon in mind when he said, "Keep deception and lies far from me, give me neither poverty nor riches; feed me with the food that is my portion, lest I be full and deny Thee and say, 'Who is the Lord?' Or lest I be in want and steal, and profane the name of my God" (vv. 8–9; NASB). The love of money can lead us to forget God.

2. Stop trusting God

One of the great dangers in having money is that you begin to trust in it. You say, "Hey, everything is great in my life because I've got my bank account built up. I'm not worrying about anything happening because I've got money for a rainy day." Now wait a minute; is that trusting the Lord?

a) Job 31:24–25, 28*b*—"If I have put my trust in money, if my happiness depends on wealth. . . . it would mean that I denied the God of heaven" (TLB). If I depend on my money, then I've denied God.

b) Proverbs 11:28—"Trust in your money and down you go! Trust in God and flourish as a tree!" (TLB).

c) 1 Timothy 6:17–18—"Charge them that are rich in this age, that they be not high-minded, nor trust in uncertain riches but in the living God, who giveth us richly all things to enjoy; that they do good, that they be rich in good works, ready to distribute, willing to share." The rich should not be proud, nor should they flaunt their riches. It is also interesting that sometimes the more money people have, the less money they're willing to part with. What they ought to do is lay up in store for themselves a good foundation against the time to come. They ought to start looking toward eternal values.

3. Be deceived

When we love money, Satan really uses that to deceive us. Listen to what it says in Mark 4:19: "And the cares of this age, and the deceitfulness of riches, and the lusts of other things entering in, choke the word, and it becometh unfruitful." When we think we have money, we think we have everything.

4. Compromise biblical instruction

Have you ever thought about what your price is? What will you sell out for? Somebody said that when money speaks, the truth is silent. For instance, some people would sell out for position. There are people on a job who would lie to get a promotion— and some are Christians. Some people would sell out for popularity. They mute the testimony of Jesus so they won't be unpopular. That's selling out.

What's your price? Have you ever analyzed it? Beloved, whatever your price is, Satan is going to get there and make you an offer at that price. So be ready. Some people would sell out for intellectualism. Some people would sell out for the body beautiful. Some people would sell out for golf, or hunting, or a new car. What's your price? I hope you don't have a price. I hope you don't compromise biblical principles to make a sale, because that's sin. I hope you don't compromise the testimony of Jesus Christ to gain a promotion. If you do, then you're selling out for the love of money.

Now you may say, "But what is the point where I sell out?" It's when Matthew 6:33 stops operating. It says, "But seek ye first the kingdom of God, and his righteousness, and all these things shall be added unto you." When you start seeking something besides the kingdom and the righteousness of God, you've sold out. Be as honest as honest can be in every single way possible.

5. Rest on unstable foundations

When you start trusting money, then you are trusting in something that passes by fast. Proverbs 23:4–5 states, "Do not weary yourself to gain wealth, cease from your consideration of it. When you set your eyes on it, it is gone. For wealth certainly makes itself wings, like an eagle that flies toward the heavens" (NASB). Don't rest on the unstable foundations of money.

6. Be ungrateful

   Deuteronomy 8 speaks of God's provision for Israel. God then warns them to beware when they are rich lest they "forget the Lord your God" (v. 14; NASB).

7. Be proud

   a) Proverbs 28:11*a*—"Rich men are conceited" (TLB). Money can make you proud.

   b) Jeremiah 12:2—"Thou has planted them, they have also taken root; they grow, they have even produced fruit. Thou are near to their lips but far from their mind" (NASB). That's hypocrisy. They said, "Thank you, God, for what You've given," but God wasn't truly in their thoughts.

8. Rob God

   When you love money you want it for yourself, and then you steal from God. Malachi 3:8 says, "Will a man rob God? Yet ye have robbed me. But ye say, How have we robbed thee? In tithes and offerings." Now you may say, "I'd never steal anything from God." But if you keep back what you should give Him, then you've robbed God.

9. Rob others

   First John 3:17 says, "But whosoever hath this world's good, and seeth his brother have need, and shutteth up his compassions from him, how dwelleth the love of God in him?" The result then is that you rob your brother.

So, the whole issue with money is attitude, and the wrong attitude is to love it. The right attitude is this: All money is God's, and since I am a steward of it, I should glorify God with all that He has given me.

III. THE WAY TO GIVE MONEY

First of all, we must recognize that the money given us is a stewardship. First Corinthians 4:2 says, "Moreover it is required in stewards, that a man be found faithful." Just think about this: During your lifetime God will entrust a lot of money to you. If you started earning fifteen thousand dollars a year at age twenty, and earned it till you were sixty, that would be over one-half million dollars. Would you be able to look back on your one-half million dollars and say that you spent all of it purposefully? Now not all of it would be used directly for the Lord's work, but would it have been used purposefully, to meet your needs and to be available to the Spirit of God? The basic principle behind this is found in 2 Corinthians 8:5 where Paul says regarding the Macedonian Christians, "But they first gave themselves to the Lord"

(NASB). This is where it all begins: we first give ourselves to the Lord, and He'll take care of the rest.

Now the Lord wants us to give to those in need, and He wants us to give to the work of Jesus Christ. We should also be careful to invest our dollars for God where He will get the best return. But remember this: *Giving is not God's way of raising money—giving is God's way of raising children.* Besides, God doesn't need our money. But every time we give sacrificially, we give a little of our selfishness away and God is praised.

Let's look at some aspects on giving.

A. Giving Should Be in Response to Need

In Acts 4 it says that the people sold their possessions, took the moneys, "and laid them down at the apostles' feet; and distribution was made unto every man according as he had need" (v. 35). Ever since the formation of the church, the money of the believers was designed to come into the church. The church leaders would then invest it in eternity as they met the needs. Now that doesn't mean that we're not to supply one another's needs without going through the church, but the dominant practice in the early church was to bring it to the church and they would distribute it.

In Acts 11:27–29 it says, "And in these days came prophets from Jerusalem unto Antioch. And there stood up one of them named Agabus, and signified by the Spirit that there should be great famine throughout all the world. . . . Then the disciples, every man according to his ability, determined to send relief unto the brethren who dwelt in Judea." Here was sensitivity to need. They heard about a need, they had a margin, and they said, "We'll all give according to our own ability." We, also, must be sensitive to needs. From time to time we hear of needs—a missionary, a brother in the church, or a neighbor—and we should go and supply those needs. So giving should be in response to need.

B. Giving Should Be in Response to God's Command

This is not specifically directed at need, but at systematic, purposeful giving. For example, it says in 2 Corinthians 9:7a, "Every man according as he purposeth in his heart, so let him give." In other words, between you and God, you need to determine what you're going to give. You say, "How do I do it?" Well, 1 Corinthians 16:2a says, "Upon the first day of the week let every one of you lay by him in store, as God hath prospered him." In other words, bring it in and give it to those in responsibility in the church, and they will invest it for eternity.

C. Giving Should Be Sacrificial

People always ask me, "John, how much should I give?" I don't know how much you should give, because that's between you and God. But I'll give you a hint: Zacchaeus, when he was saved, gave fifty percent for a starter (Luke 19:8). Now I don't think that's the norm, but it sure shoots down the ten-percent theory. I do not believe that you'll find tithing in the New Testament. Every time the New Testament has an opportunity where it could interject the ten percent, it makes sure it never does—because we're not under law, we're under grace. Besides, if you check the Old Testament carefully, tithing is at least twenty-three percent a year and up—not ten percent.

Now when we give it should be sacrificial. David said, "Neither will I offer burnt offerings unto the Lord my God of that which doth cost me nothing" (2 Sam. 24:24*b*). That means sacrifice.

D. Giving Should Be Secret and Humble

The Pharisees liked to announce how much they were giving, but Jesus said that you should be quiet and humble, and let it be between you and God. That's the spirit of giving. Matthew 6:1–4 says, "Take heed that ye do not your alms before men, to be seen by them; otherwise ye have no reward of your Father, who is in heaven. Therefore, when thou doest thine alms, do not sound a trumpet before thee, as the hypocrites do in the synagogues and in the streets, that they may have glory from men. Verily I say unto you, They have their reward. But when thou doest alms, let not thy left hand know what thy right hand doeth, that thine alms may be in secret; and thy Father, who seeth in secret, shall reward thee openly." If you give for the sake of men, then you will get their praise, and not God's. In other words, make it a secret. Jesus illustrated this by using a hyperbole: "Don't even let one hand know what the other hand is doing." That's how secret it ought to be.

E. Giving Is the Key to Spiritual Fruit

Jesus said in Luke 16:10–11: "He that is faithful in that which is least is faithful also in much; and he that is unjust in the least is unjust also in much. If, therefore, ye have not been faithful in the unrighteous money, who will commit to your trust the true riches?" If you don't handle your ten dollars properly, you wouldn't handle a million properly. So if you can't handle money properly, you won't be able to handle that which is really valuable. Some people say, "I don't know why I don't have a ministry, and I don't know why I don't see much fruit in my life." Well, it could be that they aren't faithful with money. Verse 12 says, "And if ye have not been faithful in that which is another man's, who shall give you that which is your own?" If you haven't been faithful with God's money as a steward, do you think He's going to give you your own ministry? In fact, there are a lot of men out of the pastorate and out of the ministry for the simple reason that they couldn't handle money. God would never commit souls unto them. If you don't handle finances correctly, God will never give you a ministry because He couldn't trust you with it.

God, help us to be faithful stewards.

Focusing on the Facts

1. Who has ultimate control over all money (see p. 9)?

2. Does God condemn money (see p. 9)?

3. What does God's Word say is the primary way to obtain money (see p. 10)?

4. According to Proverbs 21:20, what does a fool do with money (see p. 10)?

5. To maintain control of your finances you must _____ ahead (see p. 12).

6. It is said that credit is fire—it's easy to start and very useful, but it can be extremely dangerous if you are careless with it. According to Proverbs 22:7b, what do you become if you are overextended with debts (see p. 12)?

7. If you are having money problems, what are at least four questions you need to ask yourself (see p. 13)?

8. The main reason we should try to get more money and become rich is so that we can give more to God. True or false (see p. 14; cf. Eccles. 5:10–11)?

9. Money is the root of all evil. True or false (see p. 15; cf. 1 Tim. 6:10a)?

10. _____ and contentment go together. So if you are not content with what you have, what's missing in your life (see p. 15; cf. 1 Tim. 6:6–7)?

11. What does *"the deceitfulness of riches"* (Mark 4:19) choke out in our lives (see p. 17)?

12. If a Christian who has sufficient resources sees another Christian in need, but fails to meet that need, what does he lack (see p. 18)?

13. Fill in the blank: In order to give properly to God, I must first give _____ to the Lord (see pp. 18–19; 2 Cor. 8:5).

14. Acts 4:35 and 11:27–29 illustrate to us that one of our primary reasons for giving is in response to _____ (see p. 19).

15. Should we give up some of our own wants and desires in order to give to God (see p. 20; cf. 2 Sam. 24:24b)?

16. According to Luke 16:10–12, will the stewardship of our money have much effect on the spiritual fruit in our lives (see pp. 20–21)?

Pondering the Principles

1. Are you like the average family who has an unexpected expense every month, but you don't expect to have one this month? What specific steps must you take to prepare for these unexpected expenses (cf. Prov. 21:20a)?

2. For most of us, the reason we have financial problems is because we have violated a biblical principle. Six violations are listed in our study: stinginess, hastiness, stubbornness, laziness, indulgence, and craftiness. Prayerfully consider these violations and their corresponding biblical references to determine if you may be guilty of any. If so, confess your sin (1 John 1:9) and turn from it. Also, memorize the applicable verses (see pp. 13–14).

3. Most of us handle money in some way every day, so it becomes easy to place our trust in it. But what if you lost everything? Would you lose all hope? Would you commit suicide? Or would you trust God to guide you and provide for you? Are you really trusting in God today? Search your heart to determine where you have placed your trust (cf. Job 31:24–25, 28b; Prov. 11:28; 1 Tim. 6:17–18).

2
Concerning the Collection— Part 1

Outline

Introduction
A. The Context of Poverty
B. The Commitment of Paul
   1. Galatians 2:9–10
   2. Romans 15:25–27
C. The Condition of Jerusalem
   1. The Poverty of Jerusalem
   2. The Persecution of the Saints
   3. The Population Explosion of Christians
   4. The Paucity of Food
D. The Conflict Between Jew and Gentile

Lesson
I. The Purpose of Giving
   A. To Support the Needy in the Church
   B. To Support the Leaders of the Church
      1. Philippians 4:15–16
      2. 1 Corinthians 9:1, 4–7, 11
      3. 1 Timothy 5:17

II. The Period of Giving
   A. Weekly Stewardship
   B. Weekly Sensitivity

Introduction

In chapter 15 of 1 Corinthians, Paul discusses that great event of history—
the resurrection of the dead. He tells us of this magnificent truth and ends
the discourse by saying that on the day when the trumpet sounds, our bodies
will become like Jesus Christ's. But then he says, *"Now concerning the
collection"* (1 Cor. 16:1a). All of a sudden he brings us down to where
we live. It's most interesting to see the apostle Paul come off such a

grandiose concept and then talk about something so mundane as the collection. But as we think about it, that is the perfect illustration of how Christianity operates. Every glimpse we ever get of future glory is only given to us to encourage us to a deeper commitment to our responsibility here and now. That's the essence of scriptural looks into the future. The whole idea of seeing ahead is to render us responsible here and now.

For example, in 2 Peter 3:11–13, Peter says, "Seeing, then, that all these things shall be dissolved, what manner of persons ought ye to be in all holy living and godliness, looking for and hasting unto the coming of the day of God, in which the heavens, being on fire, shall be dissolved, and the elements shall melt with fervent heat? Nevertheless, we, according to his promise, look for new heavens and a new earth, in which dwelleth righteousness." A glimpse into the future lays great responsibility on the present. When the Spirit of God, in 1 Corinthians 15, shows us the fantastic reality of resurrection day, it has a tremendous impact on the way we live right now, even how we put our money in the collection. After all, if this body is going to leave this world and be transformed, then we shouldn't be so concerned about investing our money in temporary things. Instead, we ought to be laying it aside for God's forever kingdom.

Jesus essentially said the same thing: "Lay not up for yourselves treasures upon earth, where moth and rust doth corrupt, and where thieves break through and steal, but lay up for yourselves treasures in heaven, where neither moth nor rust doth corrupt, and where thieves do not break through nor steal; for where your treasure is, there will your heart be also" (Matt. 6:19–21). Investing in forever is the issue. If you're going to be glorified in the future, there's no sense in blowing a lot of money on unnecessary things. You might as well invest in forever.

Now let's look at some background information regarding the collection.

A. The Context of Poverty

In the ancient world, poverty was a live issue because many people were so poor. Now we seldom see that degree of poverty in our country. There are places in the world today where poverty is like it was in biblical times, but our society knows very little of that kind of poverty. In ancient times, poverty was such a serious issue in that part of the world that society itself had taken some steps to deal with it. For example, among the Greeks there were associations known as *eranoi*. These were associations of people that banded together to provide interest-free loans for people who couldn't meet their needs. The Jews did the same thing. In the synagogues there were officials who had the responsibility to determine who would receive the funds earmarked for welfare.

So it was common among the pagan Greeks and it was common

among the Jews to meet the needs of their poor. The church could certainly do no less if it was to defend its theology of love. We're in a similar situation today because in our society the government takes care of the welfare needs. But I'm afraid that very often the church is a little hesitant to do what it needs to do to meet the needs of its own people. I think sometimes we take advantage of the government opportunity when we ought to be giving in the name of Jesus Christ. We're very fortunate that the government does provide, but where it can't or doesn't, the church must be ready and eager to share.

B. The Commitment of Paul

1. Galatians 2:9-10—"And when James, Céphas, and John, who seemed to be pillars, perceived the grace that was given unto me, they gave to me and Barnabas the right hands of fellowship, that we should go unto the Gentiles, and they unto the circumcision. Only they would that we should remember the poor; the same which I also was diligent to do."

The poverty situation resulted in a strong commitment from Paul. When Paul first began his ministry, he was called by the Lord Jesus. But later on he visited Jerusalem and received an official commission from Peter, James, and John. They sent Paul and Barnabas to the Gentiles and told them to remember the poor. Now in 1 Corinthians 16 Paul says the collection of money was "for the saints" (v. 1a). What saints? Well, it is the saints at Jerusalem because in verse 3b he says, "Will I send to bring your liberality unto Jerusalem." But why? Because there was an abundance of poor Christians in Jerusalem. They had a real poverty problem there, so Paul was collecting money to take to the poor saints at Jersualem.

2. Romans 15:25-27—"But now I go unto Jerusalem to minister unto the saints. For it hath pleased them of Macedonia and Achaia to make a certain contribution for the poor saints who are at Jerusalem. It hath pleased them, verily; and their debtors they are. For if the Gentiles have been made partakers of their spiritual things, their duty is also to minister unto them in carnal things."

In other words, if the Gentiles have benefited because of God's spiritual work through Israel, the Jews should benefit because of God's giving an abundance to the Gentiles economically. Now what does he mean by that? He simply means this: Salvation is of the Jews insofar as the whole Old Testament came through them (John 4:22)—as well as most of the New

Testament. Jesus Himself was a Jew. In a sense then, the Gentiles have been made partakers of that which was given to the Jews. So Paul says, "If the Jews' possession of spiritual things has been dispersed to the Gentiles, then the Gentiles' possession of carnal things, or money, should be dispersed back in an attitude of thanks." So Paul took the collection as a thank offering to the Jews to meet their extreme need at that point in time.

C. The Condition of Jerusalem

Now why was it that the saints in Jerusalem were poor? Well, I think there are at least four reasons why they were so poor.

1. The poverty of Jerusalem

Jerusalem in the time of Solomon was rich, but in the time of Jesus and Paul it was poor. Not only that, it was grossly overpopulated because it was such a religious mecca. Numerous people came into the city and many of them stayed. Consequently, it caused a certain amount of drain on the city's economy. To make matters worse, when feast time came, the city was literally drowned in people. As many as two million additional people could arrive in the city at a feast time. So there was always a strain on the resources of Jerusalem. In fact, in those days, Jerusalem was largely dependent upon the gifts of Jews who traveled abroad and made large fortunes. They would send back money as a benefaction to be dispersed among the poor and as a contribution to the Temple. So Jerusalem was poor, and it was dependent upon gifts.

2. The persecution of the saints

The Christians in Jerusalem were poor because they were persecuted for their faith in Christ. They weren't even able to get a job in many cases. Plus, none of those Jewish benefactors who were granting money to the city would want it to go to those who were confessing a crucified, rejected Messiah. In fact, the book of Acts through chapter 8 and 1 Thessalonians 2:14 tell of the persecution of the saints in Jerusalem.

3. The population explosion of Christians

When the church was born on the Day of Pentecost, it was born at a time when the city was literally exploding with people. No doubt many of the people who received Christ in those early days were pilgrims from other cities, but after they became Christians, they stayed in Jerusalem. They stayed because that was the location of the new church, and they then lived in the homes of other Christians. Something had to be provided for them, so there was an immediate drain upon the resources of the church. Acts 2:44b says that they "had all things common." When somebody had a need, then somebody else met it. Well, after a while this became difficult, and by the time you come to the end of chapter 4 it's evident that they had drained their resources to the point that they had to sell their properties. This couldn't go on forever because they would run out of land. So as you see the church moving through the book of Acts, you see a continuing drain on the church's resources.

4. The paucity of food

Another reason I believe they were poor in Jerusalem was because of the famine in the land. In fact, the church at Antioch, which was the first church founded outside Jerusalem, sent some gifts with Paul to those who were poor in Jerusalem (see Acts 11:27–30).

So there are the reasons for the basic poverty problem of the saints in Jerusalem. Now because of the need in Jerusalem, and in response to the instruction of Peter, James, and John to remember the poor, Paul spent over a year collecting money. He wrote to the Corinthians to ask them to have a part in this collection, and this was not the first time they had heard about it. It's evident to me that they had even asked him about it. That's why he begins by saying, "Now concerning the collection" (1 Cor. 16:1a). First Corinthians was written in response to a letter from the Corinthians asking about various issues, and here Paul responded to their questions regarding the collection.

Paul gave the Corinthians instruction that has provided principles for the church throughout history as to how the church should best receive its funds. Now these are not commands by God, but they are patterns given by Paul, which form a very good basis for the church's giving even today. Paul said that he would get the whole collection together and deliver it to the Jews in Jerusalem. And that's precisely what he did. In Acts 24:17 he says, "Now after many years I came to bring alms to my nation, and offerings." Paul apparently took a number of years to collect all the money for Jerusalem.

D. The Conflict Between Jew and Gentile

Now what Paul was doing was not just sociological, it was also theological. Paul knew there was a basic dichotomy between Jew and Gentile. The Jerusalem church was Jewish, and the churches in Asia Minor, Achaia, Macedonia, Galatia, and other parts of the world were Gentile. In his heart, Paul always had this consuming passion to see the Body of Christ become one. In fact, he wrote in Ephesians 2:14 about the unity of the Body and how the Jew and Gentile should be one. He wanted "one in Christ" to be a reality. Paul realized that maybe there was one great way that he could do that. He could, in a sense, accomplish two things in one act. By relieving the needs economically of the Jerusalem church, through that overwhelming act of love, the money from the Gentiles would go a long way to solidify unity. For example, if there's somebody that I meet who has a need, my act to meet that need is not only sociological, but it invariably gains a response of love. Paul knew that. He could see that if the Gentile church would just reach out in love and meet the Jewish need, it would go a long way to bring about unity.

It is interesting to note that several times in the New Testament when Paul refers to the collection, he calls it the *koinōnia* (see Rom. 15:26; 2 Cor. 9:13). Now the word *koinōnia* means "fellowship." But to Paul there was no separation; you cannot share money without having fellowship. So that's what he saw as he took the offering to the Jewish Christians from the Gentile churches —a great opportunity for them to repay a great spiritual debt in an act of overwhelming love.

Now, let's begin to look at the principles outlined here for receiving the collection.

Lesson

I. THE PURPOSE OF GIVING (v. 1)

"Now concerning the collection for the saints, as I have given order to the churches of Galatia, even so do ye."

Paul gave us some basic directives here for Christian giving that go beyond the occasion in Corinth. In fact, I think that's why the Holy Spirit put them here—so they would have an impact on our giving today. But what was the purpose of giving in this passage? It was "for the saints" in Jerusalem. It's the same collection that Paul mentioned to the Galatians, the Macedonians, the Achaians, and in those in Asia Minor. Now he tells the Corinthians about it. But notice that the purpose was "for the saints." Now this may not have been the only purpose for this collection, but as you study the New Testament you will find that the primary purpose for all collections was to benefit the church. In Acts 2:44b they "had all things common"; in Acts 4:32c "they had all things common"; then in Acts 6:1-3 they are distributing food to the widows. So the church is to invest in its own life and its own people.

Now that does not mean that we are to have nothing to do with people outside the church, because in Galatians 6:10 the apostle Paul says, "As we have, therefore, opportunity, let us do good unto all men, especially unto them who are of the household of faith." So we are to do good to all men. A good example is the story of the Good Samaritan who went out of his way to minister to a Jew even though he came from a different culture and a different religion (Luke 10:25–37). This is indicative to me that there are times when God wants us to do good to those who are not of the household of faith.

But Paul's point in this passage is that the church's primary responsibility is to make sure that it funds its own needs. Notice also, that it is not one local church funding only itself, but one local assembly in Corinth caring for the needs of another local assembly in Jerusalem. So, when the church understands what it is universally, it will meet its needs anywhere, as well as meeting its local needs.

Now let's look closer at the purpose of giving. Giving is necessary.

A. To Support the Needy in the Church

As Christians we are to give to support those among us who are poor and needy. In other words, we give to meet the needs of people, whoever they are. There are people in our church who from time to time have their needs met as we supply what they don't have. Actually, the church in Paul's day had a great advantage over us. They didn't have to do a lot of building, so their moneys could be poured back into the lives of the people to meet their physical needs, as well as their spiritual needs. Just as Paul's offering was not only an act of sociological welfare, but of love and unity as well, so too we are to give money to meet spiritual needs as well as physical needs.

Hebrews 13:16 says, "But to do good and to share forget not; for with such sacrifices God is well pleased." And Jesus is quoted in Acts 20:35b as saying, "It is more blessed to give than to receive." It is a basic Christian truth that there is great blessing as we give to support those who have need in the church.

B. To Support the Leaders of the Church

Christians are not only to support the people in their church, but their leaders as well. In fact, on a number of occasions the apostle Paul received collections for himself.

1. Philippians 4:15–16—Paul responds to the Philippians by thanking them for the offering they gave him: "Now ye Philippians know also that in the beginning of the gospel, when I departed from Macedonia, no church shared with me as concerning

29

giving and receiving, but ye only. For even in Thessalonica ye sent once and again unto my necessity." In other words, Paul said that they supported him. And he had every right to that support because he was a leader in the church.

2. 1 Corinthians 9:1, 4–7, 11—Paul says, "Am I not an apostle? Am I not free? Have I not seen Jesus Christ our Lord? Are not ye my work in the Lord?" Then continuing in verse 4: "Have we no right to eat and to drink? Have we no right to lead about a sister, a wife, as well as other apostles, and as the brethren of the Lord, and Cephas? Or I only, and Barnabas, have we no right to forbear working?" In other words, Paul says, "Do I have the right to eat and drink? Do I have the right to have a wife? Do I have the right to have a coterie of people to minister with me? Do Barnabas and I have the right to stop working so that we can do this job? If I have these rights, then somebody will have to pay me."

Paul continues this thought in verse 7: "Who goeth to war any time at his own expense? Who planteth a vineyard, and eateth not of its fruit? Or who feedeth a flock, and eateth not of the milk of the flock?" Even Moses said in the law, "Thou shalt not muzzle the ox when he treadeth out the grain" (Deut. 25:4). If you want the ox to tread the grain, let him eat a little as he goes. Paul states a basic principle here. Then he says, "If we have sown unto you spiritual things, is it a great thing if we shall reap your carnal things?" (v. 11). In other words, "If we give you spiritual food, then you need to provide for us in return."

3. 1 Timothy 5:17—Now this is a most interesting verse: "Let the elders that rule well be counted worthy of double honor, especially they who labor in the word and doctrine." This is another verse that deals with the financing of the ministry. Now the term "elder" is a synonym for pastor, or bishop, or presbyter. Any of those terms are used for leaders in the church. Now notice that of the elders in the church, some of them rule well, which means that there may be differences in how effectively they minister. This passage says that there are some who rule well and labor especially hard in the Word and doctrine. Now the Greek indicates that those who labor with great diligence are worthy of double pay. So not only is the church to support its leadership, but it is to do so with respect to how diligently its leadership works.

So the church is called upon to support its people and its leaders. For me, one of the great joys of receiving from the church is the joy of giving back—not only in a spiritual sense, but giving back into God's church some of what God's church has given me financially.

II. THE PERIOD OF GIVING (v. 2)

"Upon the first day of the week let every one of you lay by him in store, as God hath prospered him, that there be no gatherings [collections] when I come."

The word *collections,* or "gatherings," is the same as the word in verse 1, *logia.* Paul didn't want to take any collections when he came because it was to be taken care of on the first day of the week.

How Did We Go from the Sabbath to Sunday?

Now the normal day for the church to meet was the first day, and it all started on Jesus' resurrection day. John 20:19 says, "Then the same day at evening, being the first day of the week, when the doors were shut where the disciples were assembled for fear of the Jews, came Jesus and stood in the midst, and saith unto them, Peace be unto you." The first post-resurrection service was held on resurrection day, Sunday, which was the first day of the week. Later, in John 20:26, we are told, "And after eight days, again his disciples were inside, and Thomas with them; then came Jesus." Eight days later would be the next Sunday. ("Eight days" was an idiom meaning "one week.") The second meeting they had after the resurrection occurred was also on a Sunday, and that became the pattern.

Then as we move into the book of Acts, we again see them gathering on that day. For example, Acts 20:6–7a says, "And we sailed away from Philippi . . . and came unto them to Troas. . . . And upon the first day of the week, when the disciples came together to break bread, Paul preached unto them." So, by the time we're into Acts 20, it's the pattern of the church to meet on the first day of the week. Now, when we come to Revelation 1:10, the first day of the week has a name—it's called "the Lord's day." It's also interesting to note that the Day of Penetcost, when the church was born, was a Sunday. Furthermore, the church never celebrated the Sabbath as such. In Colossians 2:16 Paul says, "Let no man, therefore, judge you in food . . . or of a sabbath day." Romans 14:6 says basically the same thing. Plus, observance of the Sabbath is the only one of the Ten Commandments not repeated in the New Testament.

So the Sabbath was set aside in favor of resurrection day, and the church came together on the first day of the week. That's why Paul says, "Upon the first day of the week let every one of you lay by him in store." Why on the first day of the week? Because that was the day of worship.

A. Weekly Stewardship

Now I've heard some people say, "Well, I wait until the end of the year, and then I write out a big check." But that's not what God wants, because then you're only dealing with the stewardship of your money once a year. No, God wants you to deal with it every week. Do you realize that how we handle money is a barometer of our spirituality? In fact, in Luke 16:11 Jesus says, "If, therefore, ye have not been faithful in the unrighteous money, who will commit to your trust the true riches?" In other words, if we're not faithful in how we handle money, then God will never give us true riches or souls. Jesus went on to say, "Ye cannot serve God and money" (v. 13c). There are a lot of Christians who need to realize that maybe the reason they're not having a great spiritual ministry is because they haven't been faithful with the financial area of their lives. I know a man who could preach with the best of them, but he's out of the ministry because he couldn't handle money. He had no credibility, so God wasn't about to to entrust to him true riches.

God wants to use you in marvelous ways. But until you're dealing every day, and every week, with the reality that every dollar you have is a stewardship entrusted to you by God, then you haven't come to grips with what Paul is saying here. Why is it that we are to give each week rather than sporadically? Because God wants us to deal with the reality of stewardship of money moment by moment.

B. Weekly Sensitivity

Someone might say, "I only get paid once a month, does that mean I have to put a check in every week and sort of spread it out?" No, I don't want you to be legalistic about it. I believe what Paul is saying is that when you come to worship God, you can only worship Him properly and have fellowship with His people, when you have dealt with your stewardship of money. Now if you're paid every two weeks, and you only give every two weeks, you still need to be sensitive on that off week. The Spirit of God might reveal somebody to you who has a need. He may need fifty dollars, so you ought to have fifty dollars available to give to that person. You need to be ready to share every week. Even on the week that you're not giving, you need to be sensitive to the prompting of God's spirit. You see, it's not just the money you give that concerns God, it's how you use *all* the money that has been entrusted to you as a stewardship.

The purpose of giving, then, is to support the church, the people, and the leaders. Beyond that, we are to reach out to anybody we see on the way who's bleeding and has a need, whether he's a Christian or not. Now the period of giving is the first day of the week because that's when the early church did it. So when a need comes along, we won't have to shout at you and get you all worked up emotionally to make you give. We want you to learn to deal systematically, week by week, wtih stewardship, so that when there are needs, the money is available because you've been faithful.

Focusing on the Facts

1. According to Matthew 6:19–21, how important are your material possessions (see p. 24)?

2. What steps did the apostle Paul take to help the poor people of the church in Jerusalem (see pp. 25–26)?

3. Why did the saints in Jerusalem have so many needs (see pp. 26–27)?

4. According to Acts 2:44–45, how did Christians meet some of the immediate needs of other Christians (see p. 27)?

5. What was one of the steps Paul used to bring unity between Jew and Gentile (see pp. 27–28)?

6. In general, who was the collection for according to 1 Corinthians 16:1 (see p. 28)?

7. Are we only to meet the needs of other Christians (see p. 29)?

8. Fill in the blank: In Hebrews 13:16 it says that God will be pleased if we don't forget to_____ _____ and _____ (see p. 29).

9. Do faithful ministers have a right to be paid for their ministries (see pp. 29–30)?

10. When a pastor is especially faithful in the ministering of the Word, his salary normally should be decreased so that he can maintain his godliness. True or false (see p. 30)?

11. What event resulted in the changing of the day of worship from the Sabbath, or Saturday, to Sunday (see pp. 31–32)?

12. Normally, God wants us to give to the church on a weekly basis. Why (see p. 32)?

Pondering the Principles

1. *Fellowship* is a word that is often synonymous with the word *sharing*. Now we saw that the Greek word *koinōnia*, which is translated as "fellowship," is also translated as "collection." With that in mind, think about this question: Is the giving of your money or your possessions evidenced as a vital part of your fellowship with other believers in need? In fact, are you *aware* of other believers in need (see p. 28)?

2. One of the greatest joys in the Christian life is to meet the needs of another. Are you alert to the needs of those around you? Someone may need food, or a refrigerator, or a bed, or clothing. Are you willing to help to meet those kinds of needs in someone's life? If you feel some hesitation, reread "Weekly Sensitivity" (pp. 32–33) and memorize 1 John 3:17.

3
Concerning the Collection—
Part 2

Outline

Introduction
A. Money Can Be a Curse
B. Money Can Be a Blessing
   1. Haggai 2:8
   2. Deuteronomy 8:18*b*
   3. 1 Corinthians 4:7
   4. James 1:17
   5. Psalm 50:10
   6. Proverbs 22:9

Review
 I. The Purpose of Giving
II. The Period of Giving

Lesson
III. The Place of Giving
   A. The Speculation
   B. The Start
   C. The Solution
   D. The Store
   E. The Sequence

IV. The Participants in Giving
   A. The Principle
      1. Mark 12:41–44
      2. Luke 16:10–11
   B. The Pattern

 V. The Proportion of Giving
   A. Giving Before Moses
      1. Freewill giving
      2. Required giving

B. Giving from Moses to Jesus
  1. Required giving
     a) Leviticus 27:30–33
     b) Deuteronomy 12:6–17: 14:22–27
     c) Deuteronomy 14:28–29
     d) Malachi 3:10a
  2. Freewill giving
     a) Proverbs 3:9–10
     b) Proverbs 11:24–25a
     c) Exodus 25:1–2
     d) Exodus 35:5, 21; 36:5–7
C. Giving from Jesus to the Present
  1. Required giving
  2. Freewill giving
     a) 2 Samuel 24:24b
     b) Luke 6:38
     c) 2 Corinthians 9:6–8, 10
     d) Luke 19:8–9

Introduction

A. Money Can Be a Curse

The Bible contains a number of warnings about money, but perhaps they are best summarized in a statement by the apostle Paul: "For the love of money is the root of all evil" (1 Tim. 6:10a). Our Lord put it tersely when He said, *"Ye cannot serve God and money"* (Matt. 6:24c). So there's no doubt about it, money can definitely be a curse. Let me remind you of what money can do to people from one of our previous studies. For money, Achan brought defeat on the armies of Israel and death on himself (Josh. 7). For money, Balaam sinned against God and tried to curse God's people (Num. 22:5–35). For money, Delilah betrayed Samson to the Philistines (Judg. 16). For money, Gehazi lied to Naaman and Elisha, and became a leper (2 Kings 5:20–27). For money, Ananias and Sapphira became the first hypocrites in the early church, and they died on the spot (Acts 5:1–11). Judas sold the Son of God for thirty pieces of silver and damned his own soul (Matt. 26:14–16, 47–50; 27:3–10). For money, many people have been cursed. In fact, the apostle Paul said, "But they that will be rich fall into temptation and a snare, and into many foolish and hurtful lusts, which drown men in destruction and perdition" (1 Tim. 6:9). So money can be a tremendous curse.

B. Money Can Be a Blessing

The Bible also teaches us that money can be a great blessing because God actually owns all of it.

1. Haggai 2:8—God says that all the silver and gold are His.

2. Deuteronomy 8:18b—It is God who has given us the power to get wealth.

3. 1 Corinthians 4:7—The apostle Paul asks. "What do you have that you didn't receive from God?"

4. James 1:17—"Every good gift and every perfect gift is from above, and cometh down from the Father of lights, with whom is no variableness, neither shadow of turning."

5. Psalm 50:10—God owns the cattle on a thousand hills.

6. Proverbs 22:9—Money can cause us to be greatly blessed when we invest it with God.

So money can be a curse, or it can be a blessing. It all depends on the attitude we have toward it. If we have an attitude of sharing, and an attitude of giving, we will be blessed. Jesus said, "It is more blessed to give than to receive" (Acts 20:35b).

Covetousness Is a Sin Basic to Man

The Bible calls the wrong attitude toward money and possessions "covetousness," which is a dominant sin in human nature. In fact, the enjoinder not to covet is one of the Ten Commandments:

1. Exodus 20:17a—"Thou shalt not covet." Now covetousness is so basic to man that I would venture to say it's probably the first sin manifested in a child. We've all heard a child say, "That's mine!" or, "Give me that!" Covetousness is a problem we struggle with all our lives. Our society makes the problem even more difficult because it encourages covetousness. Advertisements tell us that we need this, and we need that, and we deserve all these things, and it goes on and on. So it's a tough battle. Not long ago I read about a priest who said that he had listened to confessions all his life and that he had heard confessions to every known sin—except the sin of covetousness.

So covetousness is a subtle sin and one that robs us of the liberty to give the way God wants us to give. Consequently, God cannot bless us in a way that He would like.

2. Romans 7:7–8a—"What shall we say then? Is the law sin? God forbid. Nay, I had not known sin but by the law; for I had

37

not known coveting, except the law had said, Thou shalt not covet. But sin, taking occasion by the commandment, wrought in me all manner of coveting." Paul said, "The thing that woke me up to my sinfulness was when I saw the sin of coveting and realized that I was a coveter." But later on in his life, Paul said, "I have coveted no man's silver, or gold, or apparel" (Acts 20:33). Do you know what happened? The Lord gave him victory over coveting.

We have to have the right attitude toward money, and the right attitude is not coveting. The right attitude is a liberal, free, willing, and sacrificial heart. That's what Paul is after in the first four verses of 1 Corinthians 16.

Review

I. THE PURPOSE OF GIVING (v. 1; see pp. 28–31)

We saw in our last study that giving is for the saints. We, as believers, have the primary responsibility to give to meet the needs of other believers, whether they are spiritual or physical. We are to invest and share freely of what we possess so that believers may have their needs met. We really don't own anything, we just hold it in trust—and if somebody needs it more than we do, then it's theirs. Now we also saw that we must meet the needs of the saints who lead us.

II. THE PERIOD OF GIVING (v. 2; see pp. 31–33)

We also learned that the first day of the week was the period of giving. We are to deal with stewardship and face the reality of giving weekly. God doesn't want us to store it up until some forgotten tomorrow, He wants us to be giving on a constant, systematic, week-by-week basis so that we're always facing the reality of stewardship.

Now we come to the third point:

Lesson

III. THE PLACE OF GIVING (v. 2a)

"Upon the first day of the week let every one of you *lay by him in store.*"

A. The Speculation

There have been many people who have tried to interpret the phrase "lay by him in store." They ask, "How are we to give? Are we just to keep a little bank account and dole out money to meet the needs as we see them? Are we to give our money to various organizations? Are we to actually bring all of our money to the church and let them decide? How are we to do it?"

Well, it's vital for us to understand what the phrase "lay by him in store" means, because we must know the place of giving. As early as the second and third centuries there were some commentators who interpreted this phrase as meaning a private account kept in the home or in a bank. In fact, this belief is not uncommon today. There are some fine Bible scholars who teach this view even today. They say the verse is telling each of us to lay by himself in store (since it doesn't say the church) "x" number of dollars every week. This is to build up a fund to be available for use when God calls on us. Others say, "No, the store is really the church," which I believe is true. Now I believe there is good reason to have some money in an account to be available for those needs that God brings directly to your attention. However, I believe this text teaches us to place our money primarily in the church.

B. The Start

From the earliest years of the church, the pattern of giving was that the saints would take their moneys and give them to the church leaders who would then distribute the funds. So, in a sense, giving was indirect to the need. The church leaders were the ones who would distribute the funds to meet the needs, rather than every individual simply giving money wherever he wanted.

Now let me show you how this functioned. Acts 4:34–37 says, "Neither was there any among them that lacked; for as many as were possessors of lands or houses sold them, and brought the prices of the things that were sold, and laid them down at the apostles' feet; and distribution was made unto every man according as he had need. And Joseph, who by the apostles was surnamed Barnabas . . . having land, sold it, and brought the money, and laid it at the apostles' feet." Now there we have the common practice of the early church. It was to make the church the central distribution point so the leaders of the church could then disseminate the funds to the area of need.

Now there is no statement anywhere in the New Testament about keeping private funds. We can't find any indication that such a practice was common to the early church. Rather, the moneys were deposited in the care of those who were in spiritual responsibility on the first day of the week. Then, those spiritually minded men determined the distribution of those funds.

C. The Solution

The phrase "lay by him in store," or "lay by himself in store," does not necessarily mean a private fund. In other words, "by himself" doesn't mean "beside himself in his house." It simply means that each individual, in a very personal and private way, is to determine what is to be set aside for giving. Nobody can tell you how much to set aside or how much to invest with God. That is something you determine by yourself, then you lay it in store.

D. The Store

What does the word "store" mean? Well, the Greek word for "store" is *thēsaurizō*, from which we get "thesaurus." A thesaurus is a treasury of words. So the word "store" means "treasury," or it could mean "a money box, a chest, a warehouse, or a chamber." It has a lot of meanings, but basically it's where you put your treasure or valuables. The word itself doesn't tell us anything about where this thing is, but if we study history we learn something very interesting.

In the early years of the pagan temples of Greece and Rome, the pagans would give their money and offerings at the temples. Now all the pagan temples had what was known as a *thēsauros*, or treasure box. The people would place their money in the *thēsauros*, which was the treasury of the temple. In fact, it got to be that these temples would not only receive the gifts of the people, but they would even hold their money for them. The biggest banks in the Greek world were in the temples because the people were fearful of the gods they worshiped, so nobody would rob the temple bank. It was the safest place to put a bank. In fact, they even had safe-deposit boxes in the temples.

So, the idea in terms of the cultural background is that of a treasury associated with a meeting place, or the place of worship. Naturally the use of the term *treasury* in that part of the world would have brought to mind the treasury at the house of worship. Therefore, it seems best to understand that the phrase is simply saying, "Put your money in the treasury." They would know that the treasury would be at their place of worship.

E. The Sequence

In 1 Corinthians 16:2*b* Paul says, "That there be no gatherings [collections] when I come." The word for collections is the same word that is used in verse 1. Now if the people just put their money in a private fund every week, when Paul came what would be the first thing they would have to do? They'd have to have a collection. Paul said that when he came he wouldn't have to take a special offering because it should already be available. So the very context indicates that the offerings would be collected and ready to be distributed when he arrived. Furthermore, in the first part of the verse it says, "Upon the first day of the week." If this is some private fund in the home, of what import is it to be on the first day of the week? It only makes sense if they viewed the first day of the week as the time when they came together as a church. So I think it's best to see the collection as giving to the common treasury of the local church. The church leaders then distribute the moneys as they are led by the Spirit.

You have a primary responsibility, according to the Word of God in this passage, to give systematically, week by week, some of your funds to the church. This is a practical pattern for giving and one that I believe the text is teaching. Now somebody might say, "Does that mean I should never meet the need of an individual without going through the church?" Not at all. I believe we have the responsibility, and the biblical injunction, to meet a need directly, as well as indirectly through the church. For example, 1 John 3:17 says, "But whosoever hath this world's good, and seeth his brother have need, and shutteth up his compassions from him, how dwelleth the love of God in him?" Reach out and meet his need! If you're like the Good Samaritan, and you see a man who's torn up and bleeding, don't say, "Well, I'm going to the temple now. I'll try to get a check processed and be back in three days." No, meet the person's need. But the systematic giving that regularly deals with stewardship is to be done on the first day of the week. It is entrusted to the care of the treasury of the church for distribution at the direction of the godly people who lead. By the way, that's one reason you want godly leadership in the church.

IV. THE PARTICIPANTS IN GIVING (v. 2a)

"Upon the first day of the week *let every one of you*."

The phrase "let every one of you" means that no one is exempt. Now some people might say, "Well, I can't give money, so I'll give my talent." No. "Well, I give my money to this organization," or, "I keep my money here." No, everyone is to systematically, week in and week out, place his offering in the treasury of the church for the distribution to the needs of the saints. It's a matter of stewardship.

A. The Principle

Some believers may say, "I'm very poor so I can't give." Are you sure? If you have anything, you have something to give.

1. Mark 12:41–44—"And Jesus sat opposite the treasury, and

41

beheld how the people cast money into the treasury; and many that were rich cast in much. And there came a certain poor widow, and she threw in two mites, which make a farthing [about one-fourth of a cent]. And he called unto him his disciples, and saith unto them, Verily I say unto you. This poor widow hath cast more in than all they who have cast into the treasury; for all they did cast in of their abundance, but she of her want did cast in all that she had, even all her living." Do you know what percent she gave? One hundred percent! If you have anything, you have something to give.

2. Luke 16:10–11—This is an important truth: "He that is faithful in that which is least is faithful also in much; and he that is unjust in the least is unjust also in much. If, therefore, ye have not been faithful in the unrighteous money, who will commit to your trust the true riches?" In other words, if you can't be faithful when you're poor, being rich isn't going to change your spirituality. In fact, being rich just compounds your problem. If you can't trust God when you're poor, believe me, it's going to be tough when you're rich and have all the resources you need apart from Him.

B. The Pattern

Second Corinthians 8 gives us the pattern for giving through the example of the poor who gave. It says that the Macedonians gave liberally and abundantly out their deep poverty. The reason is given in verse 5: "But first gave themselves to the Lord." Because they gave themselves to God, they then gave abundantly to Him out of their deep poverty. *If you have anything, you have something to give . . . and that's an investment with God.*

V. THE PROPORTION OF GIVING (v. 2b)

"As God hath prospered him."

What proportion of our money are we to give? The common answer is that we should give ten percent. In fact, not long ago I read a book on the subject of why we should give ten percent. Is that what we're to give? Well, let's look at Giving Before Moses, Giving from Moses to Jesus, and Giving from Jesus to the Present.

A. Giving Before Moses

1. Freewill giving

Some people say that prior to Moses the people gave a tenth. Abram gave a tenth to Melchizedek (Gen. 14:20), and Jacob gave a tenth to the Lord (Gen. 28:22). They're right. So they say, "You see, the tenth was before the Mosaic law, so it must supersede the Mosaic law and still be for today." However, it's interesting to go back and really study giving before Moses. Abram gave a tenth one time in his whole life, but we never have a record that he ever gave a tenth again. Jacob gave a tenth once also. Now these two were the only ones who ever did it, in spite of the fact that there were myriad offerings given in that time. From Cain and Abel's first offering, all the way through all of the offerings ever given before Moses, there are only two times when it was a tenth. In neither case was the tenth commanded or binding as a standard of giving for all time.

2. Required giving

   In Gensis 41 and 47 God required giving. He told the inhabitants of Egypt that there was going to be a famine. Through Joseph, God said that in order to take care of the needs of the people, he must command everyone to give one-fifth of all that the land produced (Gen. 41:34; 47:24–26). What percent is that? Twenty percent. God laid out twenty percent as a standard of giving for one reason—taxation. He was funding the government of Egypt so that it could meet the needs of its people. That was the only indication that an amount was ever prescribed in pre-Mosaic times. All other offerings were completely freewill offerings.

B. Giving from Moses to Jesus

   1. Required giving

      a) Leviticus 27:30–33—In this passage God said that the people must give a tenth of all that they had. This would be given to the Levities because they were the priests. Israel was called a theocracy because God ruled through its leaders, and the leaders were the priests. The priests were the public servants, and the tenth that was paid as the Levite tax was to provide for the public servants. This was not freewill giving; it was taxation again, because it went to fund the government.

      b) Deuteronomy 12:6–17; 14:22–27—These passages tell us that they were required to give another ten percent every year to fund the national holidays and feasts. This provided for national unity and the national religion.

      c) Deuteronomy 14:28–29—Here is a third ten percent that went to the poor. This was welfare, and it was required every third year. So ten percent, ten percent, and three and one-third percent was the annual funding for the government. The tithe was never related to freewill giving; it was required taxation.

d) Malachi 3:10*a*—"Bring all the tithes into the storehouse." The word for "storehouse" in the Hebrew means "the Temple treasury." God is saying, "Pay your taxes." In fact, it's interesting to note that the taxation for Israel was about twenty-three percent, and it was twenty percent for Egypt. What is the base of taxation in America today? Around twenty percent. So we're not too far afield from the standard that God set up a long time ago.

2. Freewill giving

Now you may say, "During the time that they were paying for the funding of the national government, was there any freewill giving? Yes, but it was over and above their taxation.

a) Proverbs 3:9–10—"Honor the Lord with thy substance, and with the first fruits of all thine increase; so shall thy barns be filled with plenty, and thy presses shall burst out with new wine."

How much were they to give? Whatever they wanted to give. They just honored the Lord and gave freely. The Lord promised that the more generous they were, the better the harvest would be.

b) Proverbs 11:24–25*a*—"There is he that scattereth, and yet increaseth; and there is he that withholdeth more than is fitting, but it tendeth to poverty. The liberal soul shall be made fat."

If you want to lose your money—hoard it. If you want to gain money—scatter it, and God will bless you richly.

c) Exodus 25:1–2—"And the Lord spoke unto Moses, saying, Speak unto the children of Israel, that they bring me an offering: of every man that giveth it *willing* with his heart ye shall take my offering."

Now this doesn't refer to one of the tithes. It was whatever they were willing to give from their hearts. That's a beautiful spirit, and that's the way it had always been. God didn't tell Abram how much to give when he was joyous; he just gave what was in his heart. God didn't tell Abel what to give; he just gave what was in his heart. God didn't tell Noah what to give when he made an offering to God after the Flood; he gave what was in his heart. And that's the same principle in this passage: Give willingly from your heart.

    d) Exodus 35:5, 21; 36:5–7—"Take ye from among you an offering unto the Lord; whosoever is of a *willing* heart, let him bring it, an offering of the Lord. . . . And they came, everyone whose heart stirred him up, and everyone whom his spirit made *willing*, and they brought the Lord's offering to the work of the tabernacle of the congregation, and for all its service, and for the holy garments. . . . And they spoke unto Moses, saying, the people bring much more than enough for the service of the work, which the Lord commanded to make. And Moses gave commandment, and they caused it to be proclaimed throughout the camp, saying, Let neither man nor woman make any more work for the offering of the sanctuary. So the people were restrained from bringing, for the stuff they had was sufficient for all the work to make it, and too much." Isn't that great? I've often thought of the day when we could come to church and say, "Folks, there will be no more offerings because we have too much." It ought to be so, because it was then. They didn't need a prescription or an amount; all they needed was a heart that was willing, and they gave. They knew they were investing with a God who couldn't be out-given. The only time the tenth ever came into play was in taxation, not in freewill giving.

C. Giving from Jesus to the Present

1. Required giving

Romans 13:6–7 says, "For, for this cause pay ye tribute also; for they are God's ministers, attending continually upon this very thing. Render, therefore, to all their dues: tribute to whom tribute is due; custom to whom custom; fear to whom fear; honor to whom honor." It doesn't say IRS, here, but the people at the IRS are God's ministers. You see, the New Testament says the same thing as the Old Testament. In the time prior to Moses, in Egypt, the standard was to pay twenty percent to the government, and give God what you wanted. In the time of Moses the people had to pay twenty-three and one-third percent to Israel, and give God whatever they wanted. What is it today? Pay your income tax as the United States prescribes it and give God whatever is in your heart to give.

2. Freewill giving

   a) 2 Samuel 24:24*b*—David said, "Neither will I offer burnt
   offerings unto the Lord my God of that which doth cost me
   nothing." Giving should be done sacrificially and magnani-
   mously. When you start giving to God, He starts to give in
   return. It's like planting seeds.

   b) Luke 6:38—Jesus gives us the pattern for giving, and rather
   than giving a figure, He gives a principle: "Give, and it
   shall be given unto you; good measure, pressed down, and
   shaken together, and running over, shall men give unto
   your bosom. For with the same measure that ye measure it
   shall be measured to you again." In other words, the only
   thing you'll get a return on is what you give. Some people
   ask me, "How much should I give?" I say to them, "How
   much do you want? How much do you want God to return
   an eternal dividend on?" Of course, you may think that
   God will just give you spiritual blessings, rather than material blessings, but that wouldn't be bad, would it?

   c) 2 Corinthians 9:6–8, 10—"But this I say, He who soweth
   sparingly shall reap also sparingly; and he who soweth
   bountifully shall reap also bountifully. Every man according as he purposeth in his heart, so let him give; not
   grudgingly, or of necessity; for God loveth a cheerful giver.
   And God is able to make all grace abound toward you, that
   ye, always having all sufficiency in all things, may abound
   to every good work." God won't just give us back the
   spiritual blessing. He'll make sure we have all sufficiency
   in all things. "Now he that ministereth seed to the sower
   both minister bread for your food, and multiply your seed
   sown, and increase the fruits of your righteousness" (v. 10).
   We will receive the physical bread and the spiritual fruits of
   righteousness by investing with God.

   d) Luke 19:8–9—There was a little man named Zacchaeus who
   was the chief tax collector, and very rich. He climbed into a
   tree to see Jesus, and Jesus invited Himself to dinner at his
   house. "And Zacchaeus stood, and said unto the Lord;
   Behold, Lord, the half of my goods I give to the poor; and
   if I have taken anything from any man by false accusation, I
   restore him four-fold. And Jesus said unto him, This day is
   salvation come to this house, forsomuch as he also is a son
   of Abraham." Zacchaeus didn't give ten percent, he gave
   fifty percent! Jesus didn't tell him to do that, but He said

that Zacchaeus was the son of Abraham in the sense that he was a spiritual son because his salvation was proved.

Jesus' statement is so true: "Ye shall know them by their fruits" (Matt. 7:16a). Likewise, John said, "But whosoever hath this world's good, and seeth his brother have need, and shutteth up his compassions from him, how dwelleth the love of God in him?" (1 John 3:17). And it's so true what James said, "Even so faith, if it hath not works, is dead, being alone" (James 2:17). You can tell a true believer because out of his heart comes this great desire to give. Zacchaeus was saved, and Jesus said it was obvious because he had a giving heart. Now if there's one thing a Christian ought to have it's a giving heart and not one that's covetous.

So what does Paul say is the proportion we are to give in 2 Corinthians 16:2? You are to give exactly what you determine to give in your heart. Paul said, "Every man according as he purposeth in his heart, so let him give, not grudgingly, or of necessity; for God loveth a cheerful giver" (2 Cor. 9:7). How much are you to give to the Lord? Whatever you want. How often are you to give to the Lord? Constantly, dealing with it on a week-by-week basis. Where are you to give to the Lord? Into the church so that it can be distributed by those who have spiritual oversight. For what reasons are you to give to the church? So that the church might support its own, to meet their needs both spiritually and physically.

Focusing on the Facts

1. By the world's standards, the vast majority of Americans would be considered rich. Fill in the blank: Even though we may not consider ourselves rich, we must still be careful not to fall "into _____ foolish and hurtful lusts" (1 Tim 6:9; see p. 36).

2. Fill in the blank: Whether or not money is a cause or a blessing in our lives is mostly dependent on our _____ (see p. 37).

3. A basic problem most people have is "keeping up with the Joneses." What sin does that attitude indicate (see p. 37)?

4. What are the two basic views on the meaning of the phrase "lay by him in store" (see pp. 38–39)?

5. What was the pattern of giving for the early church in regard to where they gave (see p. 39)?

6. What does the word "store" (1 Cor. 16:2) mean? Does knowing the meaning help us to determine where we are to give (see p. 40)?

47

7. Does all the money we set aside to meet the needs of others have to go to the "store" (see p. 41)?

8. How does our faithfulness concerning money affect our spiritual riches (see p. 42)?

9. Fill in the blank: In order to have a proper attitude about giving, we must first give _____ to the Lord (see p. 42).

10. Did God command Abraham and Jacob to give ten percent (see pp. 42–43)?

11. In Genesis 41 and 47 God required a certain percentage in giving. What was it (see p. 43)?

12. Moses commanded the people of Israel to give various tithes. What was the approximate percentage they were to give per year (see pp. 43–44)?

13. In Exodus 25:2 and 35:5, 21 there's no mention of a percentage, but it does indicate a necessary attitude in giving. What was it (see pp. 44–45).

14. If you cheat on your income tax, whom have you actually cheated (see p. 45)?

15. According to Luke 6:38, what benefit do you receive when you give generously (see p. 46)?

16. If a person who claims to be a Christian never gives to his local church or to meet the need of others, it is quite likely that he is not a true believer. What are two Scriptures that give us insight into this possibility (see p. 47)?

Pondering the Principles

1. Covetousness most often reflects a person's desire for something he doesn't have, which can become a consuming sin. Think about this: Is there something that you have a constant desire to possess? Is it something you can desire or obtain without sinning? Have you sought God's wisdom on the matter (see pp. 37–38)?

2. Read Mark 12:41–44 and note the attitude of the poor widow. It's obvious that she trusted in the faithfulness of God and His provision. Does your giving reflect your faith in God's provision? Or does it reveal your anxiety about tomorrow (see pp. 41–42)?

3. In 2 Samuel 24:24 David tells us that giving should be sacrificial. Do you have this in mind when you are in the process of determining what you should give to God or to someone in need?

4. Second Corinthians 9:6 uses two contrasting words to describe giving. Which word best describes your giving? If you are not satisfied with your answer, what steps must you take to change it?

4
Concerning the Collection—
Part 3

Outline

Introduction
A. God Has Commanded Compassion for the Poor
   1. Exodus 20:2
   2. Deuteronomy 26:5–8*a*
   3. Amos 2:6–8
      a) Sold the righteous
      b) Oppressed the poor
      c) Immortality
      d) Idolatry
   4. Amos 5:11–12
   5. Amos 6:4–6
   6. Amos 7:11, 17
   7. Isaiah 10:1–4
   8. Jeremiah 5:26–29
   9. Jeremiah 34:17
  10. Psalm 146:5–9*a*
  11. Proverbs 14:31*a*
  12. Proverbs 19:17
B. God Identifies with the Poor
   1. Luke 4:18–19
   2. Matthew 25:31–45
      a) The nations separated
      b) The righteous separated
      c) The unrighteous separated
   3. Matthew 8:20
   4. 1 Samuel 2:7–8*a*
   5. Luke 1:52–53
C. God Blesses the Poor
   1. 1 Corinthians 1:26–28
   2. James 2:2–6*a*
D. God Deals with the Rich

1. The rich who are blessed
   a) 2 Corinthians 8:9
   b) 1 Timothy 6:17–19
2. The rich who are cursed
   a) James 5:1–4
   b) Jeremiah 22:13–19*a*

Review

Introduction

First Corinthians 16:1–4 is a text that deals with the objective to meet the needs of the poor saints in Jerusalem. The apostle Paul had a burning desire to collect an offering from the Gentile churches, who were somewhat wealthy, in order to give it to the poor saints in Jerusalem who were in dire need. Now the Corinthians knew about this, but they had some questions as to how Paul wanted the collection to be made. He responded in this letter, with these four verses as instructions to the Corinthians concerning their part in the collection. However, these instructions go far beyond the specific situation in the Corinthian church. They can be broadened to teach us principles of giving that are as far reaching and poignant for us today as they were for the Corinthians. Behind this whole issue is the need to meet the dire distress of poor people. Now I want to give you the divine attitude of God that's behind the heart of Paul in meeting the needs of the saints in Jerusalem.

A. God Has Compassion for the Poor

   1. Exodus 20:2—As far back as the Exodus, when God first called out His people, we can see His attitude toward His poor and oppressed people. In this text, the preamble to the Decalogue (the Ten Commandments), God identifies Himself in this way: "I am the Lord thy God, who have brought thee out of the land of Egypt, out of the house of bondage." In other words, God sees Himself as a liberating God, as a God who frees people from bondage; who frees people from poverty, from slavery, from depression and oppression.

2. Deuteronomy 26:5–8a—Moses said, "And thou shalt speak and say before the Lord thy God, A Syrian ready to perish was my father, and went down into Egypt, and sojourned there with a few, and became there a nation, great, mighty, and populous." In other words, a few people went into Egypt, but they came out a nation. "And the Egyptians badly treated us, and afflicted us, and laid upon us hard bondage; and when we cried unto the Lord of our fathers, the Lord heard our voice, and looked on our affliction, and our labor, and our oppression. And the Lord brought us forth out of Egypt with a mighty hand." Now the whole point Moses is making here is that God redeemed the people out of poverty, and bondage, and slavery, and oppression, and need. God has always identified closely with the people when they were in great distress.

3. Amos 2:6–8—What is sad about Israel is that they were scattered and destroyed for doing to the poor among their own people exactly what the Egyptians had done to them. The kingdom was divided after Solomon, and Israel was split into two parts: the Northern Kingdom with ten tribes and the Southern Kingdom with two tribes—Judah and Benjamin. The Southern Kingdom was known as Judah, and the Northern Kingdom was called Israel. They existed coequally for a while with unmitigated evil in the north, and evil and good mixed in the south. Finally, in 722 B.C., the Northern Kingdom was scattered into oblivion. The reasons are given in Amos: "Thus saith the Lord: For three transgressions of Israel, and for four, I will not turn away its punishment" (v. 6a). Now here are the reasons:

a) They sold the righteous—"Because they sold the righteous for silver" (v. 6b). For money they would sell a righteous man.

b) They oppressed the poor—"And the poor for a pair of shoes, that pant after the dust of the earth on the head of the poor, and turn aside the way of the meek" (vv. 6b–7a). They would do anything to step on the neck of the poor. If they could get just a pair of shoes, they would sell the poor.

c) They committed immorality—"And a man and his father will go in unto the same maid, to profane my holy name" (v. 7b).

d) They were involved in idolatry—"And they lay themselves down upon clothes laid to pledge by every altar, and they drink the wine of the condemned in the house of their god."

Notice that one of the reasons was the way they oppressed the poor.

4. Amos 5:11–12—"Forasmuch, therefore, as your treading is upon the poor, and ye take from him burdens of wheat: ye have built houses of hewn stone, but ye shall not dwell in them; ye have planted pleasant vineyards, but ye shall not drink wine of them. For I know your manifold transgressions and your mighty sins; they afflict the just, they take a bribe, and they turn aside the poor in the gate from their right." Once again, they had oppressed the poor.

5. Amos 6:4–6—In this passage we are told what the rich became in their oppression of the poor. "[They] that lie upon beds of ivory, and stretch themselves upon their couches, and eat the lambs out of the flock, and the calves out of the midst of the stall; that chant to the sound of the harp, and invent to themselves instruments of music, like David; that drink wine in bowls, and anoint themselves with the chief ointments; but they are not grieved for the affliction of Joseph." They didn't care about the poor or those who where trodden down. They just became fatter and fatter.

God really indicted the rich—not because they were rich, but because they had become rich at the expense of the poor. When God established Israel He said that at the end of every seventh year they had to release all the slaves (Ex. 21:2), and at the end of every fiftieth year they had to return property to its original owner (Lev. 25:28). Do you know why? So nobody could really stack it up. If a person obtained a piece of land from a poor person in the forty-eighth year, two years later it went back to its original owner. Consequently, God maintained a close gap between the rich and the poor. But all of a sudden we see Israel begin to pile up a lot of possessions and ignore the seven year release, and no doubt the fiftieth year release as well. The rich got richer, and the poor got poorer. They ground the poor in the dirt. So God said that He was going to wipe them out.

6. Amos 7:11, 17—"For thus Amos saith, Jeroboam shall die by the sword, and Israel shall surely be led away captive out of their own land. . . . Therefore, thus saith the Lord: Thy wife shall be an harlot in the city, and thy sons and thy daughters shall fall by the sword, and thy land shall be divided by line, and thou shalt die in a polluted land; and Israel shall surely go into captivity away from his land." Do you see what hap-

pened? Israel went back into captivity for doing the very same thing the Egyptians had done to them.

7. Isaiah 10:1–4—Now the same thing happened to the Southern Kingdom. One hundred years before the Southern Kingdom went into captivity a prophet came along by the name of Isaiah. He could see what was happening, and he predicted the inevitable: "Woe unto them who decree unrighteous decrees, and who write grievousness which they have prescribed, to turn aside the needy from justice, and to take away the right from the poor of my people, that widows may be their prey, and that they may rob the fatherless! And what will ye do in the day of visitation, and in the desolation which shall come from far? To whom will ye flee for help? And where will ye leave your glory? Without me they shall bow down under the prisoners, and they shall fall under the slain. For all this his anger is not turned away, but his hand is stretched out still." In other words, God said, "Because of what you've done to the poor, and because of your oppression of the needy, I'm going to take you into captivity." Isaiah saw this one hundred years before it happened.

8. Jeremiah 5:26–29—One hundred years from the time of Isaiah, another prophet, by the name of Jeremiah, was there when the captivity occurred. He also saw the inevitable: "For among my people are found wicked men; they lie in wait, as he that setteth snares; they set a trap, they catch men. As a cage is full of birds, so are their houses full of deceit; therefore they are become great, and grown rich. They are grown fat, they shine; yea, they pass over the deeds of the wicked; they judge not the cause, the cause of the fatherless, yet they prosper; and the right of the needy do they not judge. Shall I not punish them for these things? saith the Lord: shall not my soul be avenged on such a nation as this?" Jeremiah saw it, Isaiah saw it, and in 586 B.C. it came to pass. The Southern Kingdom went into Babylonian captivity for the oppression of the poor, the very thing from which they themselves had been freed when God brought them out of Egypt.

9. Jeremiah 34:17—"Therefore, thus saith the Lord, Ye have not hearkened unto me, in proclaiming liberty, every one to his brother, and every man to his neighbor. Behold, I proclaim a liberty for you, saith the Lord, to the sword, to the pestilence, and to the famine; and I will make you to be removed into all the kingdoms of the earth." They weren't releasing the slaves every seventh year. So Israel and Judah were scattered because they oppressed the poor.

10. Psalm 146:5–9a—"Happy is he that hath the God of Jacob for his help, whose hope is in the Lord, his God; who made heaven, and earth, the sea, and all that therein is; who keepeth truth forever; who executeth justice for the oppressed; who giveth food to the hungry. The Lord looseth the prisoners; the Lord openeth the eyes of the blind; the Lord raiseth those who are bowed down; the Lord loveth the righteous; the Lord preserveth the sojourners; he relieveth the fatherless and widow." That's the kind of God we have. He's not only a creator. He's a lover of the poor, and the needy, and the widows, and the orphans.

11. Proverbs 14:31a—"He that oppresseth the poor reproacheth his Maker." When you oppress the poor by not paying him a fair wage, or by not sharing your abundance to meet his need, then you reproach God. Why? Because God cares for that poor person.

12. Proverbs 19:17—"He that hath pity upon the poor lendeth unto the Lord, and that which he hath given will he pay him again." When you withhold from the poor, you mock God. When you give to the poor, you invest with God and He will pay you back.

B. God Identifies with the Poor

1. Luke 4:18–19—God came into this world in the form of a man, but His great heart for the poor and needy wasn't any different. When Jesus arrived in Nazareth at the beginning of His ministry in Galilee, He stood up in the synagogue and opened the Scripture to Isaiah. Luke recorded what He said: "The Spirit of the Lord is upon me, because he hath anointed me to preach the gospel to the poor; he hath sent me to heal the broken-hearted, to preach deliverance to the captives, and recovering of sight to the blind, to set at liberty them that are bruised, to preach the acceptable year of the Lord." Did you notice how He identified with the poor and the needy? God always does.

2. Matthew 25:31–45

a) The nations separated—"When the Son of man shall come in his glory, and all the holy angels with him, then shall he sit upon the throne of his glory. And before him shall be gathered all the nations; and he shall separate them one from another, as a shepherd divideth his sheep from the goats. And he shall set the sheep on his right hand, but the goats on the left" (vv. 31–33). Here's the judgment of the nations at the return of Jesus.

Now let's look at the criteria for judgment.

b) The righteous separated—"Then shall the King say unto them on his right hand, Come, ye blessed of my Father, inherit the kingdom prepared for you from the foundation of the world; for I was hungry, and ye gave me food; I was thirsty, and ye gave me drink; I was a stranger, and ye took me in; naked, and ye clothed me; I was sick, and ye visited me; I was in prison, and ye came unto me. Then shall the righteous answer him, saying, Lord, when saw we thee hungry, and fed thee; or thirsty, and gave thee drink? When saw we thee a stranger, and took thee in; or naked, and clothed thee? Or when saw we thee sick, or in prison, and came unto thee? And the King shall answer and say unto them, Verily I say unto you, Inasmuch as ye have done it unto one of the least of these my brethren, ye have done it unto me" (vv. 34–40). The criterion for judgment here is how they treated the least among those in the family. When we treat someone who is poor, and naked, and hungry, and in prison, with kindness and love, and meet his need, we have done it unto Christ. Do you see how inextricably identified God is with people in need?

c) The unrighteous separated—"Then shall he say also unto them on the left hand, Depart from me, ye cursed, into everlasting fire, prepared for the devil and his angels; for I was hungry, and ye gave me no food; I was thirsty, and ye gave me no drink; I was a stranger, and ye took me not in; naked, and ye clothed me not; sick, and in prison, and ye visited me not. Then shall they also answer him, saying, Lord, when saw we thee hungry, or athirst, or a stranger, or naked, or sick, or in prison, and did not minister unto thee? Then shall he answer them, saying, Verily I say unto you, Inasmuch as ye did it not to one of the least of these, ye did it not to me" (vv. 41–45). God identifies with the poor and oppressed.

When God came into the world, did He come to a palace? Did He come in a fancy robe? Did He walk on a red carpet? No. When our Lord Jesus came into His world, He was born in a small and insignificant village: "But thou, Bethlehem Ephrathah, though thou be little among the thousands of Judah, yet out of thee shall he come forth unto me that is to be ruler in Israel" (Mic. 5:2*a*). Jesus was also born to an obscure family—Joseph and Mary. He was born in a borrowed stable, and His first visitors were animals and shepherds. His parents were too poor to bring a lamb for an offering when they went for the purification at the Temple after His birth, so they had to bring two pigeons (Luke 2:22–24). That was a gift of the poorest of the poor. He was a teacher of Judaism, and teachers of Judaism were very poor. God identified with the poor.

3. Matthew 8:20—"And Jesus saith unto him, The foxes have holes, and the birds of the air have nests, but the Son of man hath not where to lay his head." The only home Jesus ever knew was a borrowed home—that of Mary, Martha, and Lazarus. Otherwise, He slept on the side of a hill. The one thing He did own was His cloak—and they gambled for that at the cross. Even in incarnation God identified with the poor.

If we go all the way back to when God chose a nation, we find that He chose one in slavery that was totally oppressed. When God wanted to choose a special people to do special things, He got tremendous joy out of picking nobodies to become somebodies.

4. 1 Samuel 2:7–8a—A dear lady by the name of Hannah couldn't believe that God was going to use her. God was going to give her a son by the name of Samuel. So she said this: "The Lord maketh poor, and maketh rich; he bringeth low, and lifteth up. He raiseth up the poor out of the dust, and lifteth up the beggar from the refuse, to set them among princes, and to make them inherit the throne of glory." Hannah said that she was a beggar and low, but God lifted her up among princes. God loves to do that.

5. Luke 1:52–53—When God chose a mother for the Messiah, He chose Mary from among the poor. After God told her of the Son she would have, she said, "He hath put down the mighty from their seats, and exalted them of low degree. He hath filled the hungry with good things; and the rich he hath sent empty away." Mary said that God is in the business of reversing the trends in the world. When God wanted a people for His name, He chose some poor slaves in Egypt. When God wanted a great man, Samuel, He chose a poor woman. When God wanted to come into the world in human form, He chose a lowly woman named Mary.

C. God Blesses the Poor

1. 1 Corinthians 1:26–28—Paul said, "For ye see your calling, brethren, how that not many wise men after the flesh, not many mighty, not many noble, are called; but God hath chosen

the foolish things of the world to confound the wise; and God hath chosen the weak things of the world to confound the things which are mighty; and base things of the world, and things which are despised, hath God chosen, yea, and things are not, to bring to nothing things that are.'' God identifies with the poor, and the common, and the needy, and the oppressed. He exalts His name by lifting them up to the level of princes, and makes them kings and priests. What a blessing!

2. James 2:2–6a—In God's church God wants us to keep His perspective. James says, "For if there come unto your assembly a man with a gold ring [i.e., a rich man], in fine apparel, and there come in also a poor man in vile raiment, and ye have respect to him that weareth the fine clothing, and say unto him, Sit thou here in a good place; and say to the poor, Stand thou there, or sit here under my footstool, are ye not then partial in yourselves, and are become judges with evil thoughts? Hearken, my beloved brethren, Hath not God chosen the poor of this world to be rich in faith and heirs of the kingdom which he hath promised to them that love him? But ye have despised the poor.'' God is in the business of picking the poor to bless. We might as well realize that if we want to identify with God, we had better identify with the poor and needy.

D. God Deals with the Rich

1. The rich who are blessed

Now God also calls some rich people. We need some rich people to share with some poor people. In fact, in the Old Testament there were some really rich people. Job was rich, but God made him poor. Then God made him richer than he had ever been. Abraham was rich; Isaac was rich; Jacob and Joseph were rich; David was rich; Solomon was rich. Then in the New Testament, Joseph of Arimathea was rich, and he was a disciple; Barnabas was rich enough to sell some land to give to poor people; Cornelius was rich; Paul met all kinds of wealthy people in his travels, and he was pleased that they were wealthy. There were many wealthy people, and they were needed in the church so they could share their wealth. But what the Bible condemns is the rich's getting richer by oppressing the poor.

a) 2 Corinthians 8:9—The greatest example of somebody who is rich and shares His wealth is God. "For ye know the grace of our Lord Jesus Christ, that, though he was rich, yet for your sakes he became poor, that ye through his poverty might be rich.'' There's nothing wrong with being rich, unless you refuse to share your riches.

b) 1 Timothy 6:17–19—''Charge them that are rich in this age, that they be not highminded, nor trust in uncertain riches, but in the living God, who giveth us richly all things to enjoy; that they do good, that they be rich in good works, ready to distribute, willing to share, laying up in store for themselves a good foundation against the time to come, that they may lay hold on eternal life.'' If the rich never share, they may never have eternal life.

2. The rich who are cursed

a) James 5:1–4—''Come now, ye rich men, weep and howl for your miseries that shall come upon you. Your riches are corrupted and your garments are moth-eaten. Your gold and silver are rusted, and the rust of them shall be a witness against you, and shall eat your flesh as it were fire. Ye have heaped treasure together for the last days. Behold, the hire of the laborers who have reaped down your fields, which is of you kept back by fraud, crieth; and the cries of them who have reaped are entered into the ears of the Lord of Sabaoth.'' In other words, God said, ''In My ears comes the cry of the workers that you underpaid to get rich.'' If you're an employer, opt out on the side of generosity. Figure out what your employees need to live on and give them more, lest their cries enter the ears of God.

b) Jeremiah 22:13–19a—There was an awful king in the Old Testament by the name of Jehoiakim. Jeremiah indicted him by saying, ''Woe unto him who buildeth his house by unrighteousness, and his chambers by wrong; who useth his neighbor's service without wages, and giveth him not for his work'' (v. 13). He was going to build himself a palace, and since he was the king, he could get the workers to do it for nothing. ''Who saith, I will build myself a wide house and large chambers, and cutteth out windows; and it is paneled with cedar, and painted with vermilion. Shalt thou reign, because thou closest thyself in cedar? Did not thy father eat and drink, and do justice and righteousness, and then it was well with him? He judged the cause of the poor and needy; then it was well with him. Was not this to know me? saith the Lord'' (vv. 14–16). He forgot that if he really wanted to be happy in life, he shouldn't have oppressed the poor to

58

get fat. He didn't act righteously like his godly father, Josiah, did.

Jeremiah continued to say, "But thine eyes and thine heart are not but for thy covetousness, and for shedding innocent blood, and for oppression, and for violence, to do it. Therefore, thus saith the Lord concerning Jehoiakim, the son of Josiah, king of Judah, They shall not lament for him, saying, Ah, my brother! or, Ah, sister! They shall not lament for him, saying, Ah, lord! or, Ah, his glory! He shall be buried with the burial of an ass" (vv. 17–19a). That's pretty straight stuff! God is not happy with people who get rich at the expense of others. Be fair and share, for God identifies with the poor.

Review

Now let's go to 1 Corinthians 16 and finish our study of these verses. Remember that the Jerusalem Christians were poor and Paul was collecting an offering for them. The Corinthians had asked how they were supposed to share, so he gave them four verses of instruction.

I. THE PURPOSE OF GIVING (v. 1; see pp. 28–31)

Giving is primarily for the saints. We are to give for their physical need and for their spiritual need. Sometimes we are to give to the saints in the pew, and sometimes we are to give to those who minister to us. First of all, we give to the Christian family, and then we are to give to anyone who has a need. God loves the stranger too and wants us to meet his need.

II. THE PERIOD OF GIVING (v. 2; see pp. 31–33)

Our giving is to be on "the first day of the week" (v. 2a). It is to be systematic, week after week, so that we come to grips with the stewardship of money.

III. THE PLACE OF GIVING (v. 2a; see pp. 38–41)

First Corinthians 16:2a also says, "Let every one of you lay by him in store." We learned that the "store" is the assembly of the church. So we are to systematically give into the store, or the treasury, when the church comes together on the first day of the week. The money is then dispensed by godly men.

IV. THE PARTICIPANTS IN GIVING (v. 2a; see pp. 41–42)

Now who is to participate in this giving? Again in verse 2a, "Let every one of you." Everybody! Nobody is exempt from systematic, week-by-week giving. It is to be a spontaneous, cheerful response of a loving heart toward a God who has given us everything. And it doesn't matter how much we have, everybody is to give.

V. THE PROPORTION OF GIVING (v. 2b; see pp. 42–47)

How much are we to give? "As God hath prospered him" (v 2b). There's no amount or percentage indicated here. Out of what God has given us do we give. You say, "Well, how do I know what to give if it's not ten percent?" Just remember that whatever you give is invested with God. Second Corinthians 9:6 says, "He who soweth sparingly shall reap also sparingly and he who soweth bountifully shall reap also bountifully." So when you're deciding how much to give, decide how much you would like a return on. Luke 6:38a states, "Give, and it shall be given unto you; good measure, pressed down, and shaken together, and running over, shall men give into your bosom." Whatever you give, God will multiply it and give it back to you. Remember also Proverbs 19:17: "He that hath pity upon the poor lendeth unto the Lord, and that which he hath given will he pay him again." So I don't know what the amount is, but I know this: Whatever God has given you, out of that you invest with God.

Now, not only should giving be an investment, but it should also be sacrificial. David said, "Neither will I offer burnt offerings unto the Lord my God of that which doth cost me nothing" (2 Sam. 24:24b). The widow gave one hundred percent (Mark 12:42–44), Zacchaeus gave fifty percent (Luke 19:8), and the Macedonians gave liberally out of their deep poverty (2 Cor. 8:2). Paul commends the Philippians for their abundant giving and tells them not to worry because God will supply all their needs according to His riches in Christ (Phil. 4:15–19). Remember too that your giving will be a measure of your spiritual overflow. Paul said that the Macedonians first gave themselves (2 Cor. 8:5), and out of that came the flow of their gift. So your giving should reflect your dedication to God. Now, let's look at:

VI. THE PROVOCATION FOR GIVING (v. 2c)

"Upon the first day of the week [give] . . . that there be no gatherings [lit., 'collections'] when I come."

Paul didn't want giving to be provoked by an emotional appeal when he arrived. He wanted it to be in the flow of faithful, week-by-week giving. It should be in the flow of life, not as the result of some emotional appeal on a periodic basis. Christians need to learn this because so many Christians do not know the meaning of systematic, week-by-week, sacrificial, generous giving. They wait for some kind of a spiritual goose bump or emotional "zap" from some appeal; then

60

they give. So, they don't understand the meaning of faithfulness in their giving. Now there are times when we should give to meet a need immediately, and that's exciting; but that's over and above our normal giving. Those opportunities are something beyond the normal flow of systematic faithfulness.

VII. THE PROTECTION IN GIVING (v. 3)

"And when I come, whomsoever ye shall approve by your letters, them will I send to bring your liberality unto Jerusalem."

Paul says, "Once you've given the money, I'm going to put it in the hands of some people that you've approved along with accompanying letters that state their trustworthiness." Money given to the church is to be cared for by approved men who are godly. That's the protection in the church. You say, "But what does that have to do with the church?" Just this: I believe that as you give systematically and faithfully into the treasury of the church, it is incumbent upon the church to choose godly men to care for God's funds.

In the early church, who was it that handled all the money? The apostles did (Acts 4:35). The people didn't give the money to somebody who didn't have the spiritual qualification to handle it. They didn't give it to the bankers or to the people with the finance background or to the businessmen. They gave it to the godly men. Now later, the apostles became so busy that they said, "Wherefore, brethren, look among you for seven men of honest report, full of the Holy Spirit and wisdom, whom we may appoint over this business. But we will give ourselves continually to prayer, and to the ministry of the word" (Acts 6:3 – 4).

But what do you see in a lot of churches? Two boards. The deacons, who handle the spiritual matters, and a group of financial people to handle the money. So when the deacons determine what God wants to do, they have to let the other board decide if they can support it financially. That doesn't make sense. Did you ever know of anything God wanted to do but couldn't because He didn't have enough money? No.

The principle here is that the funds should be put in the hands of the godliest people in the church. Paul says, "Look, you find the people that have proved trustworthy, get the letters of approval together, and I'll send them with the money." Let the money be entrusted to godly men who prayerfully, in the energy of the Holy Spirit, determine its distribution. That's the protection in giving.

VIII. THE PERSPECTIVE IN GIVING (v.4)

"And if it be suitable that I go also, they shall go with me."

Paul said, "Listen, if you give enough so that I won't be embarrassed, I'll accompany it. But I'm not about to take a long trip to Jerusalem if you just give a little bit." Paul wanted them to stretch themselves. At the end of verse 3 he says, "Them will I send to bring your liberality unto Jerusalem." The word for "liberality" is *charis* in the Greek, meaning "your grace, your overabundance, your generosity." When we give, we are to give generously.

Now we've learned that God identifies with those who have need, so we want to give our money to those in physical need, to those in spiritual need, and to support those who minister to us. I don't know about you, but God has given me a whole new sense of responsibility to those who don't have anything, or to those who have less than I do. Listen, we can't do any less than give because of all that God has given to us. God made the sun—it gives. God made the moon—it gives. God made the stars—they give. God made the air—it gives. God made the clouds—they give. God made the earth—it gives. God made the sea—it gives. God made the trees—they give. God made the flowers—they give. God made the beasts—they give. God made man—does he give?

May it be said of us what was said by the Lord Jesus: "But when you give alms, do not let your left hand know what your right hand is doing" (Matt. 6:3, NASB). Give in secret and let God openly reward you.

The Mark of a Christian

Writing in about A.D. 125, a Christian philosopher by the name of Aristides looked at Christianity and said this: "They walk in all humility and kindness, and falsehood is not found among them, and they love one another. They despise not the widow, and grieve not the orphan. He that hath, distributeth liberally to him that hath not. If they see a stranger, they bring him under their roof, and rejoice over him, as it were their own brother: for they call themselves brethren, not after the flesh, but after the spirit and in God; but when one of their poor passes away from the world, and any of them see him, then he provides for his burial according to his ability; and if they hear that any of their number is imprisoned or oppressed for the name of their Messiah, all of them provide for his needs, and if it is possible that he may be delivered, they deliver him. And if there is among them a man that is poor and needy, and they have not an abundance of necessaries,

> they fast two or three days that they may supply the needy with their necessary food." Isn't that great!

I hope we'll take what the Scripture has taught us and apply it to our lives. I want God to show us where we need to make changes so that we may give of the riches He has given to us.

Focusing on the Facts

1. According to Deuteronomy 26:5–8a, what was the reason God brought the children of Israel out of Egypt (see pp. 50–51)?

2. What was one of the main reasons Israel was taken into captivity (see p. 51)?

3. Why did God want Israel to release its slaves at the end of seven years and to return property to the original owner after fifty years (see p. 52)?

4. Fill in the blank: God became _____ because of Israel's treatment of the poor (see p. 53; Isa. 10:4).

5. According to Psalm 146:5–9, what does God do for those in need (see p. 54)?

6. Did you know that you can give a loan to the Lord? What do you have to do to make that loan and to receive it back with interest (see p. 54; Prov. 19:17)?

7. If we give to someone in need, who are we actually giving to (see p. 55)?

8. How is Jesus' entry into the world as a baby identified with the poor (see p. 55–56)?

9. Should there be any separation between the poor and the rich in the church (see p. 57)?

10. The rich will be blessed only if they perform what acts (see pp. 57–58)?

11. What will happen to those employers who hold back fair wages to become rich (see p. 58)?

12. What was Jehoiakim's fate because of his oppression of the poor (see pp. 58–59)?

13. We should give only when we feel a special leading of God. True or false (see pp. 60–61)?

14. In order to run the church these days, most of the leadership must have special knowledge of finances. True or false (see p. 61)?

Pondering the Principles

1. In Matthew 25:31–45 we have the account of Christ's separating the

nations at the advent of the kingdom. The criterion for judgment is how they treated the needy—whether or not they met their need. Reread the passage, and then think of what your first reaction is to someone in need. Do you have any fears or reluctances? If you do, why? Meditate on 1 John 3:17–18 (see pp. 54).

2. One of the greatest proofs to the world that we are Christians is our love for one another (cf. John 13:35). In the Greek, *agapē* is the purest kind of love, and it is based on action, rather than feeling. Now our best example of this kind of love is Jesus Christ Himself. When He sacrificed Himself for us, He proved that His love was not just a feeling He had for us (cf. Eph. 5:1–2). This same type of love is seen in the actions listed by Aristides in "The mark of a Christian" (see p. 54). Now reread this portion carefully, and observe how they sacrificed themselves for one another. Could any of these things be said of you? Are there any of these deeds that you are unwilling to do? If there are, think over carefully what it really means to be a committed Christian, and read 1 John 4:7–21 *several* times.

5
God's Plan for Giving— Part 1

Outline

Introduction
A. How We Feel About Money
    1. We are not to love it
    2. We are not to trust it
    3. We are not to seek to be rich
    4. We are not to regard it as our own
B. How We Earn Money
    1. The negatives
       a) Don't steal it
       b) Don't exploit others by usury
       c) Don't defraud people by not paying them
       d) Don't gamble for it
    2. The positives
       a) By receiving gifts
       b) By making wise investments
       c) By work
C. How We Spend Money
    1. By poviding for our family
    2. By paying our debts
    3. By saving

Lesson
I. Giving Before Moses
    A. Freewill Giving
       1. Tithe: its meaning
       2. Tithe: it's not commanded
       3. Tithe: its use
          a) Abraham
          b) Jacob
    B. Required Giving
       1. Genesis 41:34
       2. Genesis 47:24

II. Giving from Moses to Jesus
   A. Required Giving
      1. Leviticus 27:30–33
      2. Deuteronomy 12:6–7
      3. Deuteronomy 14:28–29
      4. Leviticus 19:9–10
      5. Nehemiah 10:32–33
      6. Exodus 23:10–11
      7. Deuteronomy 15:1–2, 9
   B. Freewill Giving
      1. Numbers 18:12
      2. Proverbs 3:9–10
      3. Proverbs 11:24–25
      4. Exodus 25:1–2
      5. Exodus 35:4–10, 21–22*a*; 36:5–7
      6. Deuteronomy 16:17
      7. 1 Chronicles 29:9, 16

Introduction

In this study we are going to discuss the subject of money because it's a problem we have to deal with all the time. Money is also a good barometer on our spirituality, because the way we handle our money is an indication of our Christian stewardship of life. More than any other single commodity, money is in our hands. We pay bills constantly, we write checks, we receive paychecks, we go to the bank, we take our wallets out, we put change in this or that, and so on. So the stewardship of money is a critical area of life, and the Bible has much to say about it.

Now Christians are faced with many decisions regarding money, and basically they fall into four categories: how we feel about money, how we earn money, how we spend money, and how we give money.

   A. How We Feel About Money

      1. We are not to love it

         First Timothy 6:10*a* says, "For the love of money is the root of all evil." We are not to love money, and that's not easy since it's around us all the time.

      2. We are not to trust it

         This means that we are not to put our confidence in our money. First Timothy 6:17*a* says, "Charge them that are rich in this age, that they be not highminded, nor trust in uncertain riches." To trust in money is idolatry. Even when we derive a sense of security from the money God provides for us, it can still lead to idolatry. Matthew 6:24 says, "No man can serve two masters. . . . Ye cannot serve God and money." That kind of divided allegiance doesn't please God. That's why when the Bible lays down the qualifications for an elder it says that he cannot be a man who is greedy of money (1 Tim. 3:1–3).

3. We are not to seek to be rich

Christians are to seek to honor God. If He desires to make us rich, that's His business. We are to seek to work as hard as we can and do the best we can for His glory. First Timothy 6:9 says, "But they that will be rich fall into temptation and a snare, and into many foolish and hurtful lusts, which drown men in destruction and perdition."

4. We are not to regard it as our own

The money we have is God's, and we are stewards of it.

B. How We Earn Money

1. The negatives

    a) Don't steal it

    We are not to steal money. But you say, "I would never do that." Listen to Psalm 37:21*a*: "The wicked borrows and does not pay back" (NASB). You see, there are lots of ways to steal. In fact, in Amos 8:5 and Hosea 12:7, the prophets condemn those who falsify the balances owed and then deceive somebody out of money.

    b) Don't exploit others by usury

    In other words, we are not to overcharge desperate people. If our brother has a need, we are to give to meet his need. Don't loan him what he needs and then charge him high rates of interest (Lev. 25:35–37; Ps. 15:5).

    c) Don't defraud people by not paying them

    James 5:4 says the money a person owes his laborers cries out against him. He defrauds them when he doesn't pay them what they deserve for their work.

    d) Don't gamble for it

    I think this is implied in Scripture from the standpoint that if you trust in the sovereignty and the providence of God, chance has no part in it. It's interesting to note that the word for "dice play," which is *sleight,* is used in connection with the ministry of Satan in Ephesians 4:14.

2. The positives

Now how are we to get money?

a) By receiving gifts

Paul received gifts constantly to meet his need (Phil. 4:10–18), and many of us have been the beneficiary of such gifts. Sometimes people send a love offering in response to a ministry that we may have had, and that is a legitimate expression of love. Now, in the Old Testament the firstborn received, in general, the inheritance of all that his father possessed. So, we can receive gifts in terms of inheritance as well as gifts of love.

b) By making wise investments

I don't believe God wants us to run the risk of wildcat investments or high-risk speculations with His funds. He desires that we make wise investments. In Matthew 25:27 the owner says to the servant, "Then you ought to have put my money in the bank, and on my arrival I would have received my money back with interest" (NASB). So we can earn money by making wise investments.

c) By work

The primary way we earn money is by good old work. The Bible says, "Six days that shalt labor, and do all thy work; but the seventh day is the sabbath of the Lord, thy God: in it thou shalt not do any work" (Deut. 5:13–14*a*). Unfortunately, many people in financial need haven't learned how to work yet. People who are chronically out of money are often chronically indolent. Now there can be extenuating circumstances, but the basic problem with people who don't have anything is that they don't work for anything. Work is a divine principle, and a lot of us like divine principles but don't get very excited about that one.

Proverbs 28:19 says, "He that tilleth his land shall have plenty of bread, but he that followeth after vain persons shall have poverty enough." A person who just floats with the crowd won't make it, but the one who works will do all right. Proverbs 14:23 is really practical: "In all labor there is profit, but mere talk leads only to poverty" (NASB). If you work, you make money—if you talk, you don't.

C. How We Spend Money

1. By providing for our families

First Timothy 5:8 says, "But if any provide not for his own, and specially for those of his own house, he hath denied the faith, and is worse than an infidel." John says in 1 John 3:17, "But whosoever hath this world's good, and seeth his brother have need, and shutteth up his compassions from him, how dwelleth the love of God in him?" So, we are to spend money to meet the needs of our households, and to meet the needs of those around us.

2. By paying our debts

We should strive to pay our debts immediately. Romans 13:8*a* says, "Owe no man any thing, but to love one another." And another verse that expands on this thought is 2 Kings 4:7*b*: "Go, sell the oil, and pay thy debt, and live thou and thy children on the rest." In other words, "Liquidate what you have to pay your debts, and live on the rest." So, we must pay our debts.

3. By saving

Did you know that there are four wise creatures in the world that God exalts? Proverbs 30:24 says, "There are four things which are little upon the earth, but they are exceedingly wise." Those creatures are ants, badgers, locusts, and spiders (Prov. 30:25–28). Now look at what Scripture says of the ant: "The ants are a people not strong, yet they prepare their food in the summer" (v. 25). They're not too strong, but they're smart enough to know that they'd better get their food in the summer because they're not going to be able to find it in the winter. Now that's saving. Proverbs 21:20 states, "There is treasure to be desired, and oil, in the dwelling of the wise, but a foolish man spendeth it up." In other words, whatever you need you will find in a wise man's treasury, but a fool has no preparation for the future. I believe that future planning is reasonable and wise, and it is biblical.

So now we've seen some of what the Bible says about how we are to spend money, how we are to earn money, and how we are to feel about money. These areas then become a barometer on our Christian lives. How we handle our wives or husbands, how we handle our kids, how we work at our jobs, how we handle relationships with other believers, how we handle our prayer life, how we handle our Bible time—all become a monitor or barometer on our spiritual lives. Money is no different. The credibility of our Christianity is manifested in the handling of our funds. Now this is a difficult area because we're constantly being bombarded by the world to spend our money stupidly. Furthermore, some Christian organizations bombard us to spend money stupidly. But our money is a qualifier of our Christianity. In a sense, that's what John means in 1 John 3:17. Our Christianity becomes manifest when we give the money we have to the person who needs it.

We have to think of the money that we have as a stewardship. If you have an employer who gives you one hundred dollars to purchase something for him, and he tells you that you will have to give an account on how you spent it, then you're going to take care of that one hundred dollars. But if you have one hundred dollars of your own then you may not feel any obligation to anybody. But whose money is it? It's God's. If you have to give an account to your employer, how much more of an account will you have to give to God for how you spend your money?

That brings us to a fourth area, which will be our main topic of discussion: *how we are to give our money.*

Christian Exploitation

Sometimes it isn't easy to keep a clear perspective on giving because we are being bombarded with constant appeals for our money. There are the solicitations for money that come in the mail, and there are half-hour religious broadcasts that spend twenty-five minutes asking for money and five minutes telling you the reasons they're asking for it. We're bombarded by techniques, giving gimmicks, church stewardship drives, budget drives, and all kinds of things. It's no wonder that Christian giving in the eyes of some people seems to be exploitation. But in the eyes of other people it seems to be totally neglected. You can take courses in certain schools on how to raise your church budget. Or you can read material on how to develop a tithing church, how to get slick things going—like loyalty week, how to have a pledge system, how to have a canvas, how to motivate people, and how to make people feel guilty because they don't do what they ought to do. Then, if you really feel desperate you can hire out-of-town experts who will come in and raise money for you for a piece of the action.

Now I'm not against stimulating people to give money; I'm just against doing it in unbiblical ways. But there are so many hucksters on TV and radio, hounding Christians for money, that the real purpose and value of giving is lost.

Many people say the solution to giving is to just accept the biblical standard of giving, which is the tithe or ten percent. They justify the ten percent by saying that if the law required ten percent, certainly grace would require at least ten percent. However, the tithe is never mentioned in the New Testament in reference to the church. But what I'm afraid they're really saying is that they know tithing is not New Testament giving, yet if they don't push the tithe, they won't get enough money to operate.

The problem with ten percent is this: (1) it isn't biblical and it's giving for the wrong reason. It's giving to fulfill an obligation rather than a response of a loving, willing heart. And (2) it hinders what you could do by making you think you're done. Giving is never to be by coercion or fund raising.

So, God's pattern for giving in the New Testament is not tithing, and it wasn't in the Old Testament either. It never has been tithing. Now this is what I want to explain to you. But let's look at some thoughts from our earlier studies and divide the history of giving into three sections: before Moses, between Moses and Jesus, and from Jesus to the present. Notice that all will teach the same pattern of giving; there is no difference.

Lesson

I. GIVING BEFORE MOSES (see pp. 42–44)

The people who teach that we should tithe, teach on the basis that because Abraham and Jacob tithed before the Mosaic law, tithing was before the law. Therefore, tithing should also be after the law. But that's like saying since the sacrificial system was actually initiated before the law, then we should go back to killing animals. I don't believe that's the idea. If we say whatever's before the law is after the law, then we will run into a lot of problems.

Giving before Moses falls into two categories, as does all giving in these periods; freewill giving and required giving. First, let's look at the book of Genesis.

A. Freewill Giving

  1. Tithe: its meaning

    The term *tithe* does appear in the book of Genesis. Now some have thought that because it appears in Genesis it becomes the standard for giving from the start. The Hebrew word *maaser*, which is translated "tithe," means "a tenth part." It's the same as *dekatē* in the Greek. It simply means "a tenth." It isn't a religious word; it's a mathematical word. It has only to do with a percentage. Historically, even outside the Bible, we know that man has always used ten as the basic number for counting systems. Ten has been the number of completion, and we see this sometimes in Scripture (e.g., ten plagues, Ex. 7:14—12:36; Ten Commandments, Ex. 20:1–17). There is also evidence that many pagan deities were honored by the giving of a tenth. Since ten represented totality or completeness, the giving of a tenth was a symbol of the giving of the whole. By the giving of what was a total number, they were simply symbolizing the fact that they were giving their all.

2. Tithe: it's not commanded

The Bible does not institute tithing in Genesis. No one told Abraham to give a tenth, no one told Jacob to give a tenth, and there's no such universal law stated in Scripture. Let me show you what I mean. In Genesis chapter 4 the first offering is mentioned. The first offering given to God stated in Scripture was from Cain and Abel. The interesting thing about it is that it was a voluntary offering. It simply says, "And in process of time it came to pass, that Cain brought of the fruit of the ground an offering unto the Lord. And Abel, he also brought of the firstlings of his flock" (vv. 3–4a). There is no command that God specifically told them to do that; at least it is not recorded in Scripture. It was a free choice on their part. Cain gave the fruit of the ground, and Abel brought an animal sacrifice. But we don't know what percentage was given. There was no requirement, no amount, no stipulation, and no frequency enjoyed upon them. It was completely at their own will.

Now in Genesis 8:15–20, after the flood subsides, Noah immediately goes out to make a sacrificial offering to God: "And Noah builded an altar unto the Lord; and took of every clean beast, and of every clean fowl, and offered burnt offerings on the altar" (v. 20). Again, it is completely voluntary. There is no command, no stipulated amount, no percentage given. Noah determined that in his own heart—it was spontaneous.

Abraham, in Genesis 12, is given the wonderful call of God to be the leader of a nation. In response to that he built an altar to the Lord (v. 7). Again, there is no command or stipulation— only the free spirit of Abraham in response to the wonderful promise of God as he says thanks by way of an offering. Abraham builds another altar to the Lord in Hebron in Genesis 13:18. So it was always a voluntary act—never in response to the command of God. These people gave to God of their own possessions out of love and thankfulness, and it was totally spontaneous. This is the pattern of freewill giving.

3. Tithe: its use

   a) Abraham

   In Genesis 14:20 we have the first mention of the tithe.
   Abram had just returned from fighting when verse 17 says,
   "And the king of Sodom went out to meet him after his
   return from the slaughter of Chedorlaomer, and of the kings
   that were with him, at the valley Shaveh." The following
   verse also says that he was met by the king of Salem. (Salem
   is the ancient name for Jerusalem.) Now the king of Salem
   was a nam named Melchizedek who was not only a king, but
   according to verse 18, "was the priest of the most high
   God" (cf. Heb. 7:1). When Abram saw this man who
   represented God, he wanted to express thanks to God for the
   victory. So it says, "And he gave him tithes of all" (v.
   20*b*). It doesn't say that God told him to do this, and it is not
   commanded that he give a tenth. Plus, I think it's interesting
   to note that it doesn't necessarily mean that he gave a tenth
   of everything that he owned. He gave a tenth of something
   that he took in this battle. In fact, Abraham lived for 160
   years, and it is not recorded in Scripture before or after this
   incident that he ever gave a tenth. This wasn't a tenth of his
   income, and it wasn't an annual tenth. It was simply that he
   chose to do it.

   Now Hebrews 7:4*b* adds another thought. It says that "Abraham, gave the tenth of the spoils." But the Greek word here
   is *akrothinion* which means "the top of the heap, the best of
   the spoils." It says that he gave him a tithe of the top of the
   heap. So it wasn't a tenth of the total pile; it was a tenth of
   the top of the pile. But the point is that it was a one-time
   thing, and there's no record that he ever gave this way
   again.

   b) Jacob

   The other use of the word *tithe* in the book of Genesis has to
   do with Jacob. In Genesis 28:22*b* Jacob says, "I will surely
   give the tenth unto thee." Now at this point Jacob was
   making a vow: "And Jacob vowed a vow, saying, If God
   will be with me, and will keep me in this way that I go, and
   will give me bread to eat, and raiment to put on, so that I
   come again to my father's house in peace; then shall the
   Lord be my God" (vv. 20–21). In other words, "God, if
   You do this, I will bow down to You." Now that's really
   bad. Jacob was at a low ebb spiritually, and what he was

doing was buying off God. Don't take this as a norm of spirituality. There's no command that he was to give a tenth—it was completely voluntary.

Now notice that from Cain and Abel right through the gift of Jacob, in all cases they were voluntary gifts. The idea that it was a tenth was arbitrary. Out of all the offerings throughout the book of Genesis, twice they happened to give a tenth, which in their eyes, and in the eyes of ancient people, simply represented the giving of all. It was nothing more.

B. Required Giving

1. Genesis 41:34

If you say that there was required giving before the Mosaic law, you're right. Now most people of that time didn't give money because their exchange was not money; it was animals, seed, or land. Now Joseph had been sold into slavery in Egypt by his brothers and eventually ended up in jail because of a false accusation in Potiphar's house. But when the Pharaoh had a dream he couldn't understand, they got Joseph to interpret the dream. He said there would be seven years of fruitful crops and seven years of famine. Joseph then suggested how they should get ready: "Let Pharaoh do this and let him appoint officers over the land, and take up the fifth part of the land of Egypt in the seven plenteous years" (v. 34). They were to tax the people at what rate? One-fifth, or twenty percent. This is the first time we find taxation of a national entity expressed in the Bible. (Notice that the amount asked for then is still the basic norm of taxation in America—twenty percent.) The basic taxation rate in Egypt was God's plan expressed through Joseph. When they collected twenty percent through the fat years, that would supply them the needed foods for the lean years. So taxation was instituted at that point and twenty percent was the figure.

2. Genesis 47:24

"And it shall come to pass in the harvest, that ye shall give the fifth part unto Pharaoh, and four parts shall be your own, for seed of the field, and for your food, and for them of your households, and for food for your little ones." Joseph says, "I'm going to leave you four parts: some to sow back into the field, some to eat, some to take care of your household needs, and some for your kids. The fifth part goes back to the government." So required giving in Genesis was twenty per-

74

cent. It was instituted in Egypt as the funding of the national government.

Now notice this: *freewill giving* is directed toward the Lord in an attitude of love and sacrifice; *required giving* is given to the national entity for the supply of the needs of the people. That's what you find from the time of creation to the time of the law.

II. GIVING FROM MOSES TO JESUS (see pp. 43–45)

Now during the time from Moses to Jesus the tithe became a familiar term, and those who teach tithing as God's universal principle lean heavily on this period for their definition.

A. Required Giving

1. Leviticus 27:30–33

   The tithe in this passage was called the Lord's tithe, or the Levite's tithe. In Numbers 18:21, 24 it tells us that this tithe was collected to be given to the Levites, who were the priests. The nation was divided into twelve tribes and one whole tribe was priests. The taxation of all the rest of the tribes went to supply the needs of the Levites. This passage in Leviticus gives us further instruction: "And all the tithe of the land, whether of the seed of the land, or of the fruit of the tree, is the Lord's: it is holy unto the Lord. And if a man will at all redeem any of his tithes, he shall add thereto the fifth part thereof. And concerning the tithe of the herd, or of the flock, even of whatsoever passeth under the rod, the tenth shall be holy unto the Lord. He shall not search whether it be good or bad, neither shall he change it: and if he change it at all, then both it and the change thereof shall be holy: it shall not be redeemed. These are the commandments, which the Lord commanded Moses for the children of Israel in Mount Sinai." In other words, you could give money in exchange for the land, the seed, and the fruit, but you could not redeem the animals. Those you *had* to give.

   So the Levite tithe was ten percent of everything that they had in terms of produce from the land and animals. Now the emphasis here was on the quantity, and it was taught that it belonged to God. This was not a freewill offering to God; it was His already. In fact, Malachi 3:8 says that they were robbing God if they didn't give the tithes and offerings. So ten percent of the animals and the produce was given to the tribe of the Levites to support them, because they didn't earn a living other than just carrying on their priestly functions.

2. Deuteronomy 12:6–7

In this passage there was a second tithe, another ten percent. It was to be taken to the central sanctuary to be eaten by the family, the servants, and the priests (v. 12). The purpose was to stimulate devotion to the Lord and to promote unity among all the people. It was like a national potluck because it made everybody share.

That brings the total close to twenty percent. They gave ten percent of everything and then ten percent of the remaining ninety percent.

3. Deuteronomy 14:28–29

"At the end of three years thou shalt bring forth all the tithe of thine increase the same year, and shalt lay it up within thy gates: and the Levite (because he hath no part nor inheritance with thee), and the sojourner, and the fatherless, and the widow, who are within thy gates, shall come, and shall eat and be satisfied; that the Lord thy God may bless thee in all the work of thine hand which thou doest."

This amount was called the poor tithe. The first percentage was called the *Levite's tithe*, the second was called the *festival tithe,* and the third was called the *poor tithe.* Now, we've got ten percent, ten percent, and three and one-third percent (that's ten percent every third year) every year. So when someone says the Jew gave ten percent, that isn't true. The Jew gave twenty-three percent to begin with. Incidentally, the third one was their welfare program. It was for the poor people, the widows, and the people who didn't have anything to eat. So they were funding the people who ran the government, which were the Levites; they were providing for national feasts through the festival tithe; and they gave for the welfare program. All this was funding for the national entity. All three of these were taxation, not freewill giving to God. Tithing was always taxation so that the programs of the government could run: the priestly program, the national religious program, and the welfare program.

4. Leviticus 19:9–10

"And when ye reap the harvest of your land, thou shalt not wholly reap the corners of thy field, neither shalt thou gather the gleanings of thy harvest. And thou shalt not glean thy vineyard, neither shalt thou gather every grape of thy vineyard; thou shalt leave them for the poor and sojourner: I am the Lord your God." This is the profit-sharing plan in Israel. They

76

didn't pick up what they dropped, and they left the corners of the field unharvested so it could be shared by the poor people.

5. Nehemiah 10:32–33

Here we see that they also had a Temple tax of one-third shekel they had to pay to buy showbread, grain, and sacrifices.

6. Exodus 23:10–11

The Jews had to have a Sabbath rest for the land every seven years, which meant that they forfeited the entire year's earnings off the land.

7. Deuteronomy 15:1–2, 9

On the same Sabbath year as the rest year, they also had to set all debts aside.

Ten percent is a long way from what it cost the Jews to exist within the theocracy of Israel. Well over twenty-five percent of their income was given to the funding of the government and to the earning of the land. That was required giving.

B. Freewill Giving

Now notice that *freewill giving* includes firstfruit giving and freewill offering. The emphasis here is not on the quantity or the percentage, but on the attitude of the giver and the quality of his gift.

1. Numbers 18:12

"All the best of the oil, and all the best of the wine, and of the wheat, the first fruits of them which they shall offer unto the Lord, them have I given thee."

This is firstfruits. The Jew would collect off the top the very best that was in the field, and then give it to God at the Temple. The beauty of this was that he hadn't harvested the crop yet so he really didn't know how much was there. He was believing God, and God was saying, "If you'll give Me the firstfruits and trust Me, I'll bring in your harvest."

2. Proverbs 3:9–10

"Honor the Lord with thy substance, and with the first fruits of all thine increase; so shall thy barns be filled with plenty, and they presses shall burst out with new wine."

There are two principles here for Israel; first, they were to honor God with every penny that they had; second, if they gave Him right off the top sacrificially, God would fill their barns, and their presses would burst out with new wine. That's

God's promise to Israel. Now God's promises to Israel were fulfilled temporarily. We cannot make the same statement for New Testament promises that are fulfilled spiritually. You say, "I knew it! I'll give it all and all I'll get in return is a spiritual blessing!" Well, we'll get into that later. But God does both: He gives spiritual blessing and He meets needs.

Now "first fruits" is giving the best of whatever you've got. Remember what God says in Malachi 1:8, 13? God says, "I'm not happy with you and I'm going to judge you because you have brought Me the blind and the lame." They were keeping the best for themselves and forfeiting His blessing. Giving to the Lord was *always* a matter of freely giving Him the best. Freewill giving isn't waiting till you've spent all your money on yourself and socked plenty away in some fund, then finally trickling a little bit to God. That isn't firstfruits. It's when you give Him the cream of what you have and keep a little bit for yourself that He'll fill your barns spiritually as well as meeting your needs physically.

3. Proverbs 11:24–25

"There is he that scattereth, and yet increaseth; and there is he that withholdeth more than is fitting, but it tendeth to proverty. The liberal soul shall be made fat, and he that watereth shall be watered also himself."

Now some people will say, "Oh, but if we do that we'll never meet the budget, and it will mess our church up because people won't tithe." If somebody believes that, then their problem isn't with me—they have a problem with the promise of Scripture.

4. Exodus 25:1–2

"And the Lord spoke unto Moses, saying, Speak unto the children of Israel, that they bring me an offering: of every man that giveth it willingly with his heart ye shall take my offering."

Now here is God's chance. All He has to say is, "I demand a tenth!" and that would seal it. But He told Moses, "I want an offering, and they can give whatever is in their heart to give." Moses didn't seem to worry about the budget because God didn't ask for a tenth.

5. Exodus 35:4–10, 21–22a; 36:5–7

"And Moses spoke unto all the congregation of the children of Israel, saying, This is the thing which the Lord commanded, saying, Take ye from among you an offering unto the Lord;

whosoever is of a willing heart, let him bring it, an offering of the Lord; gold, and silver, and bronze, and blue, and purple, and scarlet, and fine linen, and goats' hair, and rams' skins dyed red, and badgers' skins, and acacia wood, and oil for the light, and spices for anointing oil, and for the sweet incense, and onyx stones, and stones to be set for the ephod, and for the breastplate. And every wisehearted among you shall come, and make all that the Lord hath commanded. . . . And they came, everyone whose heart stirred him up, and everyone whom his spirit made willing, and they brought the Lord's offering to the work of the tabernacle of the congregation, and for all its service, and for the holy garments. And they came, both men and women, as many as were willing-hearted. . . . And they spoke unto Moses, saying, The people bring much more than enough for the service of the work, which the Lord commanded to make. And Moses gave commandment, and they caused it to be proclaimed throughout the camp, saying, Let neither man nor woman make any more work for the offering of the sanctuary. So the people were restrained from bringing; for the stuff they had was sufficient for all the work to make it, and too much.''

When people believe in the ministry, and when they believe what you're doing exalts God, they will give too much. This is a clear illustration that giving, done with true motivation, goes beyond the need.

6. Deuteronomy 16:17

''Every man shall give as he is able, according to the blessing of the Lord thy God which he hath given thee.''

Required giving was always taxation. Freewill giving was always whatever came out of the willing heart. When people believe in what you're doing, their willing hearts open up. Those people in Exodus 35 believed that it would honor God to have a tabernacle. So they poured out everything they had, and they saw it completed.

7. 1 Chronicles 29:9, 16

''Then the people rejoiced; for they offered willingly, because with perfect heart they offered willingly to the Lord; and David, the king, also rejoiced with great joy. . . . O Lord our God, all this abundance that we have prepared to build an house for thine holy name cometh of thine hand, and is all thine own.''

David wanted to build a temple, and in this passage we see

how everything was brought together for its construction. David marveled at the abundance that came in for the building of God's house, and when Solomon finally built it, it was absolutely unbelievable. The material wealth the people had provided for the building of the Temple was astounding.

Tithing was taxation for the theocracy. We don't live in a theocracy, but government is still ordained of God. And our taxation today isn't far from what they paid in those days. So we're really not too far off what God originally instituted as the basics of taxation. But that isn't giving. Don't get stuck at ten percent, and don't limit yourself to legalistic giving. Be free in the Spirit of God to give superabundantly. Sow bountifully so that you may reap bountifully (2 Cor. 9:6).

Focusing on the Facts

1. What are the cautions on how we should feel about money (see pp. 66–67)?

2. When is borrowing money considered stealing (see p. 67)?

3. What is the primary way we are to obtain money (see p. 68)?

4. If a Christian does not provide for his family he is worse than an _____ (see p. 69; 1 Tim. 5:8).

5. What does Scripture say about paying our debts (see p. 69)?

6. Who does the money you have really belong to (see p. 70)?

7. What does the word *tithe* mean in Scripture (see pp. 71–72)?

8. Was Noah commanded to give to the Lord immediately after the Flood? Does it say what the percentage was that he gave (see p. 72; Gen. 8:15–20)?

9. When Abraham gave to Melchizedek, did he give a "tithe" on all that he owned (cf. Gen. 14:17–20)? What is significant about the Greek word *akrothinion* in Hebrews 7:4b (see p. 73)?

10. Did Jacob have a proper motive in giving *"the tenth"* in Genesis 28:20–22 (see pp. 73–74)?

11. What percentage of giving did Pharaoh require from the people of Egypt on the advice of Joseph (see p. 74; Gen. 41:34; 47:24)?

12. Was the giving of the tithe to the Levites freewill giving, or required giving (see p. 75; Lev. 27:30–33)?

13. Which percentage is closest to the total amount the Jew was required to give: ten percent, or twenty-three percent (see p. 76)?

14. The best of what you give to God is called the _____ (see p. 77).

15. Did God state a percentage when He told Moses to ask for an offering in Exodus 25:1–2 (see p. 78)?

16. How many times is the word *willing* used to describe a heart attitude in Exodus 35:4–10, 21–22a? What resulted from that attitude (see pp. 78–79; Ex. 36:5–7)?

Pondering the Principles

1. Reflecting on Matthew 6:24, who would you say is your master? Who would those close to you say is your master? Who would Jesus say is your master (see p. 67)?

2. Are you wise like the ant, or do you spend all that you have foolishly (see p. 69; Prov. 30:24–25)? Are you saving to meet needs, or are you going in debt to obtain your wants? If you are not prepared for the unexpected needs (e.g., car breaks down, refrigerator quits, etc.), then maybe you should memorize and meditate on Proverbs 21:20.

3. Consider what your attitude is when you give to the Lord. Do you give grudgingly, or do you give with a willing heart? Are you expecting material benefits, or spiritual blessing? Think carefully, because your attitude will determine your usefulness to God (Luke 16:9–13).

6
God's Plan for Giving—
Part 2

Outline

Introduction

Review
I. Giving Before Moses
II. Giving from Moses to Jesus
III. Giving from Jesus to the Present

Lesson
A. Required Giving
   1. Matthew 17:24–27
   2. Matthew 22:15–22
   3. Matthew 23:23
   4. Luke 18:12
   5. Hebrews 7:4
   6. Romans 13:1–2, 6–7
B. Freewill Giving
   1. Giving is investing with God
      a) Luke 6:38
      b) Matthew 6:19–21, 24
      c) 2 Corinthians 9:6–7
      d) Matthew 19:21
   2. Giving is to be sacrificial
      a) Mark 12:41–44
      b) Hebrews 13:16
      c) Philippians 4:18–19
   3. Giving is not a matter of what you have
      a) Luke 16:10
      b) 2 Corinthians
   4. Giving affects spiritual riches
   5. Giving amounts are personally determined
   6. Giving is to be in response to need
   7. Giving is to demonstrate love, not law

8. Giving is to be planned
9. Giving is to be generous
10. Giving generously results in blessing

Introduction

Giving, like all other subjects in the Bible, is the revelation of God and it needs to be understood. The apostle Paul was able to say to the Ephesian elders: "For I have not shunned to declare unto you all the counsel of God" (Acts 20:27). Likewise, for me not to declare unto you these principles of giving would be to rob you of blessing in an area that God has allowed for such wonderful blessing. I think it's important for us to put this in perspective because I believe most Christians misunderstand the teaching of giving in the Bible.

Does Giving in Church Ever Seem Unpleasant?

If you said yes, let me give you three primary reasons why some churches would make you feel this way:

1. Preoccupation with money

   In some churches it seems everything that goes on has a dollar sign attached to it. Their success is measured on how big the offering was. Consequently, no opportunity is ever lost for making constant appeals for money, and every conceivable approach or gimmick is used to make those appeals effective. Plus, churches very often get into the area of business by marketing certain things at a profit. This is one of the things we feel strongly about at Grace Church. If we provide anything, it is provided at precisely what it cost us to make that provision. To overcharge at all would unnecessarily take money away from our congregation.

2. Partiality toward the rich

   In many churches today the wealthiest people dictate their theology and their policy. John Murray said, "Perhaps few weaknesses have marred the integrity of the church more than the partiality shown to the rich. The church has compromised with their vices because it has feared the loss of their patronage. Its voice has been silenced by respective persons, and discipline has been sacrificed in deference to worldly prestige." James said, "My brethren, have not the faith of our Lord Jesus Christ, the Lord of glory, with respect of persons. For if there come unto your assembly a man with a gold ring, in fine apparel . . . and say unto him, Sit thou here in a good place; and say to the poor, Stand thou there, or sit here under my footstool, are ye not then partial in yourselves, and are become judges with evil thoughts?'' (James 2:1–4). There's no place for partiality—only impartiality. When a church is partial to the rich it might as well be selling indulgences.

3. Pressure by spiritual fear

Now there are other churches that use spiritual fear to pressure people to give. That is equally wrong. The right thing to do about giving is to teach the truths of the Word of God and leave the response to the Spirit of God, along with the rest of the fruits of spirituality.

So we shouldn't use gimmicks or programs. Instead, we must just teach the Word of God and allow the Spirit of God to produce the kind of giving commensurate with the blessing of the Christian life.

Review

I. GIVING BEFORE MOSES (see pp. 42–43, 71–75)

II. GIVING FROM MOSES TO JESUS (see pp. 43–45, 75–80)

Now the third area we want to look at is:

III. GIVING FROM JESUS TO THE PRESENT (see pp. 45–47)

The New Testament also instructs us in giving, but it really says the same thing the Old Testament does. Some people have said, "Well, Old Testament giving was one thing, and New Testament giving is something else.'' That's not true. New Testament giving is more clearly defined, but it is the same. The two kinds of giving stressed in the New Testament are: (1) pay your taxes; (2) give God whatever you want—there is no set amount. Let's examine what the New Testament says about required giving.

Lesson

A. Required Giving

Now remember, the tithes that were exacted from the Jews— along with the Temple tax, the Sabbath rest for the land, and the special profit-sharing tax—were all taxation. In the times when the gospels were written the Jews were still under those laws. So it was proper for a Jew to continue to pay his tithes to Israel for the support of the priests, to have money for the poor, and to provide for the feast in Jerusalem. In addition, the Romans were exacting exorbitant taxes from them. But they were still under the obligation of Mosaic law to pay their taxes.

1. Matthew 17:24–27

   This passage says, "And when they were come to Capernaum, they that received tribute [tax] money came to Peter, and said, Doth not your master pay tribute? He saith, Yes" (vv. 24–25a). Jesus paid His taxes, and we ought to pay our taxes. I think it's exciting to see Matthew present this because Matthew was involved in declaring Christ as King. But even though Jesus is King of kings, He still subscribed Himself to paying the required legal taxes.

   Now look at how He paid them: "And when he was come into the house, Jesus spoke first to him, saying, What thinkest thou, Simon? Of whom do the kings of the earth take custom or tribute? Of their own sons, or of strangers? Peter saith unto him, Of strangers. Jesus saith unto him, Then are the sons free" (vv. 25b–26). In other words, Jesus said that we don't *have* to pay taxes since we're truly in the family of the King. However, He continued on to say, "Notwithstanding, lest we should offend them, go thou to the sea, and cast an hook, and take up the fish that first cometh up. And when thou hast opened its mouth, thou shalt find a piece of money; that take, and give unto them for me and thee" (v. 27). Now that's the way to get your tax money! If that was still in vogue, around April 1 the beaches would be lined with Christians. But the point of the passage is simply this: Jesus paid His taxes. Jesus advocated what the Father had advocated in the Old Testament: Pay your taxes.

2. Matthew 22:15–22

   "Then went the Pharisees, and took counsel how they might entangle him in his talk. And they sent out unto him their disciples with the Herodians, saying, Master, we know that thou art true, and teachest the way of God in truth, neither carest thou for any man; for thou regardest not the person of men [which means that Jesus didn't care for one man over another]. Tell us, therefore, What thinkest thou? Is it lawful to give tribute unto Caesar, or not?" (vv. 15–17). They were asking, "Should we pay our taxes to Rome, or not?" Now if Jesus said, "Pay your taxes," then the Jews would reject Him. But if He said, "Don't pay your taxes," then the Romans would be after Him. They thought they had Him between a rock and a hard place. "But Jesus perceived their wickedness, and said, Why test me, ye hypocrites? Show me the tribute money. And they brought unto him a denarius. And he saith unto them, Whose is this image and superscription? They say unto him,

Caesar's. Then saith he unto them, Render, therefore, unto Caesar the things which are Caesar's; and unto God, the things that are God's. When they had heard these words, they marveled, and left him, and went their way" (vv. 18–22). Taxation is necessary, and Jesus said, "Pay your taxes." That's required giving.

3. Matthew 23:23

Jesus calls the Pharisees hypocrites seven times in chapter 23: "Woe unto you, scribes and Pharisees, hypocrites! For ye pay tithe of mint and anise and cumin [i.e., little herbs, plants, and seeds] and have omitted the weightier matters of the law." Jesus didn't condemn paying the tithes, because that was their taxation system. He just told them that they ignored the things that really matter, and that's why He called them hypocrites. But notice that tithing here was in reference to required giving, not freewill giving. The tenth of everything a man possessed was to be given because this was taxation under the economy of Israel.

4. Luke 18:12

This passage is the only other reference to tithing in the gospels, and like all other passages that mention tithing in the New Testament, there is no exacting of the tithe on the church. Tithing is always mentioned in reference to Israel's economy. In Luke 18:12 it is used in connection with boasting and hypocrisy. A Pharisee came to the Temple, prayed to himself, and said, "I fast twice in the week; I give tithes of all that I possess." He was boasting about his tithing, but there wasn't anything to boast about—he was suppose to pay his taxes. Now that's all the gospels say about tithing, and all of these incidents were in reference to Israel's paying its taxations to the national government, or Rome.

5. Hebrews 7:4

This mention of tithing refers to what Abraham gave to Melchizedek. He gave a tenth; not because God told him to, but because he volunteered to give that amount. At no time does the New Testament ever suggest, or even hint, that the tithe should be exacted upon the Christian.

6. Romans 13:1–2, 6–7

Since we're not under the Jewish economy you may think, "Well, I don't have to pay my taxes anymore because that was for the funding of the national government of Israel." No, it says in Romans 13, "Let every soul be subject unto the higher powers. For there is no power but of God; the powers that be are ordained of God. Whosoever, therefore, resisteth the power, resisteth the ordinance of God; and they that resist shall receive to themselves judgment. . . . For, for this cause pay ye tribute [tax] also; for they are God's ministers, attending continually upon this very thing" (vv. 1–2, 6). You may say, "But they're not very godly!" You're right. In many cases that is true. Nevertheless, God has designed human government as a force to keep society together—to punish the evil and to support the good. In that sense, rulers govern in the place of God through an institution of God called *human government*. In other words, when you pay your taxes, you are supporting the work of God.

Now I know that comes as a shock, but it's true. You say, "But if I cheat a little on my taxes I'll get more money for the Lord." No, you will rob the Lord. You will fall into the category of Malachi 3 by not paying your taxes. So don't cheat the government, or you'll just cheat yourself out of blessing. "Render, therefore, to all their dues: tribute to whom tribute is due; custom to whom custom; fear to whom fear; honor to whom honor" (v. 7). Honor the government, and God will bless your obedience to His principle because you've supported His ministers.

So, when the New Testament speaks about required giving, it says, "Pay your taxes."

B. Freewill Giving

We come now to the category of giving that is truly giving to God. After all, there is no reference about tithing in any passage in the New Testament where it talks about Christian giving—absolutely none. Jesus never made the tithe incumbent; Paul never made it incumbent; none of the writers of the New Testament made the tithe incumbent as Christian giving.

Now let's look at the ten principles that the New Testament does give for Christian giving.

1. Giving is investing with God

a) Luke 6:38

"Give, and it shall be given unto you; good measure, pressed down, and shaken together, and running over, shall men give into your bosom." Do you see the principle there? You don't have to be a banker to figure out that it is the principle of investment. You give to God, and it will be given to you.

A good portion will be measured out and "pressed down." That means it won't be like the crackers you buy at the market that are in a little pile at the bottom of the box when you open it. But when God gives back to you it will be jam packed. You see, God will move upon others to support your needs, far beyond what you gave.

"For with the same measure that ye measure it shall be measured to you again" (v. 38b). What you invest with God, you receive dividends on; what you don't invest with God, you don't receive any dividend on. Now this is the biblical principle in the New Testament that's the basis for Christian giving. Giving is investing with God, and the return is an eternal dividend.

b) Matthew 6:19–21, 24

"Lay not up for yourselves treasures upon earth, where moth and rust doth corrupt, and where thieves break through and steal; but lay up for yourselves treasures in heaven, where neither moth nor rust doth corrupt, and where thieves do not break through nor steal; for where your treasure is, there will your heart be also." In other words, be sure that your priority is investing with God—because wherever you put your treasure, that's where you're going to put your heart.

For example, if I take $20,000 and put it in an earthly investment, do you know what I'll do? I'll start thinking about it. Everytime I get the paper I'm going to find out where the stocks are to find out about my money. I'll plug into what's happening economically and start biting my economic fingernails because I'll be worrying about my $20,000. All that does is generate my attitudes and actions toward the world because that's where I put my treasure. But if I take the same $20,000 and give it to God, then where does that generate my attention? I'll say, "Lord, remember that $20,000 I gave You? I hope You're seeing some return on it." It would generate my relationship to Him, and that's what it means when it says, "Where your treasure is, that's where your heart is going to be." For wherever your investment is, that's what you'll be preoccupied with because you'll want to see the dividends on your investment.

The point becomes very clear in verse 24: "No man can serve two masters; for either he will hate the one, and love the other; or else he will hold to the one, and depise the other. Ye cannot serve God and money." We can't be a slave to God and money—it's one or the other. If we would learn to invest with God it would generate our activity toward Him, because we'd be checking on our investment. I would much rather give my money to God than to any organization that runs on an economic basis. Only God is a secure investment.

c) 2 Corinthians 9:6–7

"But this I say, He who soweth sparingly shall reap also sparingly; and he who soweth bountifully shall reap also bountifully. Every man according as he purposeth in his heart, so let him give, not grudgingly, or of necessity; for God loveth a cheerful giver." If you give freely, God will supply your needs. He has all sufficiency to provide everything you need, both physically and spiritually. It's like going to the bloodbank to give your blood. Now that's a precious commodity, but in about thirty-six hours you have that blood back. God causes your body to reproduce it. That's the way it is spiritually. When we invest with God, He'll return it with interest.

d) Matthew 19:21

The rich young ruler came and inquired of Jesus, and "Jesus said unto him, If thou wilt be perfect, go and sell what thou hast, and give to the poor, and thou shalt have treasure in heaven; and come and follow me." Some people read that and say, "Wow, do you have to give your money away to be a Christian?" No, Jesus didn't mean that we have to give our money away to be a Christian. What He told the rich young ruler was that his money was standing between him and God.

Does Money Stand Between You and God?

There once was a slave who was a tremendous Christian and exhibited a great testimony to his master. One day his master came to him and said, "Whatever you've got, I want it. You have such peace and joy and contentment. How can I get it?" The slave said, "Go to the house, put on your white suit, and come down here and work in the mud with the rest of us slaves, then you can have it." The master said, "What are you talking about? I could never do that. I'm the master, and you're the slave. I can't do that; it's beneath my dignity." And he walked off in a huff.

The master came back a couple of months later and said, "I can't resist asking you again. What is it you have, and how can I have it?'' The slave said, ''I told you, go put your white suit on, come down and work in the mud with us, and you can have it.'' The master was furious again and walked off.

Finally, in desperation, he came back to the slave and said, ''I don't care what it takes, I've got to have it. I'll do anything.'' The slave said, ''Go, put on your white suit, and come down here with us. Will you do that?'' The master said, ''Yes,'' The slave replied. ''You don't have to.''

Do you see the point? He knew what was standing between the man and Christ: pride. That's all that Jesus said. Until a person is detached from his money, he will be separated from God, because he can't serve both.

2. Giving is to be sacrificial

   a) Mark 12:41–44

      ''And Jesus sat opposite the treasury, and beheld how the people cast money into the treasury; and many that were rich cast in much. And there came a certain poor widow, and she threw in two mites, which make a farthing [a fourth of a cent]. And he called unto him his disciples, and saith into them, Verily I say unto you, this poor widow hath cast more in than all they who have cast into the treasury; for all they did cast in of their abundance, but she of her want did cast in all that she had, even all her living.'' Now how did He know that? Because He knows everything. She only had one-fourth of a penny left and she gave it. That amount doesn't seem significant, but it was, because she gave everything. Friends, you can't give any more than everything. The point that Jesus was making is that sacrifice is the essence of giving. The ultimate sacrifice would be to give everything, and in this case, the least money was the greatest gift.

      So what does it teach about giving? Does it teach that we're to tithe? No. It teaches that we're to give sacrificially, and maybe that means everything we have. Certainly it means more than what we're giving now.

   b) Hebrews 13:16

      ''But to do good and to share forget not; for with such sacrifices God is well pleased.'' You see, what pleases God is sacrifice.

   c) Philippians 4:18–19

      Paul had just received money from the Philippians, and he

was thankful. He said to them, "But I have all, and abound. I am full, having received of Epaphroditus the things which were sent from you, an odor of a sweet smell, a sacrifice acceptable, well-pleasing to God. But my God shall supply all your need according to his riches in glory by Christ Jesus." Because they gave sacrificially, they invested with God, and Paul said that God would supply all their needs according to His riches.

3. Giving is not a matter of what you have

People always seem to say, "If I only had more, I would give more." Oh, really? I read one time about the preacher who went to visit a farmer. The preacher said, "Say, if you had two hundred dollars, would you give one hundred of it to the Lord?" The farmer said, "I would." The preacher said, "If you had two cows, would you give one of them to the Lord?" The farmer said, "I would." The preacher then asked, "If you had two pigs, would you give one of them to the Lord?" The farmer said, "Now that isn't fair. You know I have two pigs." He wasn't willing to give what he had.

Let's see what Scripture says about this principle.

a) Luke 16:10

Now we may give more in amount, but it may not be more in proportion to what we have, and proportion is what God is after. Jesus said, "He that is faithful in that which is least is faithful also in much; and he that is unjust in the least is unjust also in much." If you are not giving sacrificially with what you have, you wouldn't give sacrificially if you had more.

b) 2 Corinthians 8:1-2, 5, 7

"Moreover, brethren, we make known to you the grace of God bestowed on the churches of Macedonia, how that in a great trial of affliction the abundance of their joy and their deep poverty abounded unto the riches of their liberality." In other words, they didn't have much, but they gave liberally anyway. This was because they "first gave themselves" (v. 5). Giving is not a matter of what you have; it's a matter of the heart; it's a matter of the sacrifice that you desire to render toward God. Then Paul says in verse 7: "Therefore, as ye abound in every thing, in faith, and utterance, and knowledge, and in all diligence, and in your love to us, see that ye abound in this grace also." When we give to God we ought to abound—in the same way we abound in these other spiritual commodities.

4. Giving affects spiritual riches

One of the most sobering statements in regard to giving found anywhere in the Scripture is in Luke 16:11: "If, therefore, ye have not been faithful in the unrighteous money, who will commit to your trust the true riches?" Now that is potent! If you can't handle money, which is earthly riches, do you think God is going to give you spiritual riches to handle? *If you don't handle money wisely, you will never be given spiritual responsibility.* Verse 12 continues with this same thought: "And if ye have not been faithful in that which is another man's, who shall give you that which is your own?"

Now here's the idea: A father has a son that he wants to give his estate to, and if he's the firstborn son then he's the heir to the estate. However, the father wants to find out if his son is going to manage the estate properly, so he gives him some money that isn't his own. He watches how the son uses the money, not for the money's sake, but as a measurement of the young man's character. If the young man doesn't use the money properly, then he's disinherited and the father gets somebody else to run his estate.

That's essentially what it means in these verses. The application to us is simply this: God commits into our hands a trust; and the money we have is not ours, it's His; He gave it to you. If you do not handle that money wisely, then God sees by the evidence that you do not handle the world's riches properly, so He will never give you true riches. Spiritual responsibility may be withheld from those who cannot handle their finances. I know men personally, and there are many others, who have moved right out of the ministry altogether. God has totally removed all of their spiritual responsibility because they had reached a place where they could not handle money. Giving affects spiritual riches. *If you want God to give you responsibility in spiritual things, then you must prove that you can handle the world's goods.*

5. Giving amounts are personally determined

In Luke 19:1–8 we have the story about the man in the tree named Zacchaeus: "And Jesus entered and passed through Jericho. And, behold, there was a man, named Zacchaeus, who was the chief among the tax collectors; and he was rich. And he sought to see Jesus, who he was, and could not because of the crowd: for he was little of stature. And he ran ahead, and climbed up into a sycamore tree to see him; for he was to pass that way. And when Jesus came to the place, he looked up, and saw him, and said unto him, Zacchaeus, make haste, and come down; for today I must abide at thy house. And he made haste, and came down, and received him joyfully. And when they saw it, they all murmured, saying that he was gone to be guest with a man that is a sinner. And Zacchaeus stood, and said unto the Lord, Behold, Lord, the half of my goods I give to the poor.'' Did he give ten percent? No. He gave fifty percent! Now Jesus could have said, ''No, all you're required to give is ten percent. You keep the rest.'' But He didn't. The Lord never restricted giving to a tenth. That would have robbed Zacchaeus of blessing. Then Zacchaeus said, ''And if I have taken anything from any man by false accusation, I restore him fourfold.'' That's four hundred percent!

The point here is that giving is spontaneously done out of love and gratitude, not out of law. Our example is Jesus Christ who gave Himself: ''For ye know the grace of our Lord Jesus Christ, that, though he was rich, yet for your sakes He became poor, that ye through his poverty might be rich'' (2 Cor. 8:9). That's the pattern: the rich should become poor that others might be rich. In the context of this passage, the Macedonians were already poor, and they became destitute to make somebody else rich. Giving is to be individually determined. It's between you and God, and it is the product of a thankful and willing heart.

6. Giving is to be in response to need

Not only is giving to be spontaneous and voluntary, but giving is also to be in response to need. For example, in Acts 2:43–47, at the time of Pentecost, Christians were sharing their goods with those who had need. In Acts 4:32–37 they were selling land and taking the money and giving it to the apostles so they could give it to the needy. In Acts 11:27–30 the apostle Paul collected an offering from the churches in the Gentile world for the needy saints in Jerusalem. The saints collected money to take to the people who were in the famine, and there was no required percentage, because the giving was to be in response to need.

7. Giving is to demonstrate love, not law

Second Corinthians 8:8 says, ''I speak not by commandment, but by occasion of the earnestness of others, and to prove the sincerity of your love.'' Paul gave them all this information about giving—not as a command, but simply as a test of their love. "For ye know the grace of our Lord Jesus Christ, that, though he was rich, yet for your sakes he became poor, that ye through his proverty might be rich" (v. 9). The pattern is that love gives everything. Don't degenerate giving into legalism. Instead, demonstrate your love by how you give.

In verse 12a it says, "For if there be first a willing mind." All God wants is a willing mind; someone who wants to give. Second Corinthians 9:7 states, "Every man according as he purposeth in his heart, so let him give, not grudgingly, or of necessity; for God loveth a cheerful giver." When you put a prescription on giving, you give people a law to abide by rather than love—then you've robbed them.

8. Giving is to be planned

Paul gave his plan for giving to the Corinthian church (1 Cor. 16:1), and he said it was the same plan that he had given to the church in Galatia: "Upon the first day of the week let everyone of you lay by him in store, as God hath prospered him, that there be no gatherings when I come" (v. 2).

Now some may say, "Well, I don't give money, I give my talent, or my time, or my ideas." But that doesn't teach you stewardship of your money. Paul said "every one of you," not "some of you." All of us must weekly prepare in our hearts the amount we are to give proportionately "as God hath prospered."

Now the phrase "that there be no gatherings when I come," indicates that there should be a church budget. Otherwise, you would always have to have special offerings. We must give on a continuous basis to teach ourselves the meaning of steward-ship, so that we don't just respond to emotional needs. Giving, then, is to be done systematically, proportionately, and faith-fully as we purpose in our hearts. In fact, the word "purposeth" (Gr., *proaireō*), as it is used in 2 Corinthians 9:7, means "to set aside beforehand." So, we are to plan, pray, and prepare to give beforehand—not haphazardly.

9. Giving is to be generous

Paul said of the Macedonian Christians in 2 Corinthians 8:2b: "Their deep poverty abounded unto the riches of their liberal-ity." They were poor, but they gave generously. Notice also that the words "bounty" and "bountifully" in 2 Corinthians 9:5–6 refer to liberality. Giving is to be generous and sacrificial.

10. Giving generously results in blessing

The apostle Paul was so grateful for the generosity of the Philippian church that he said, "But I rejoiced in the Lord greatly that now at the last your care of me hath flourished again; of which ye were also mindful, but ye lacked opportunity" (Phil. 4:10). Because of their generosity, he then said, "But my God shall supply all your need according to his riches in glory in Christ Jesus" (v. 19). When you give generously, God will meet all your needs.

Second Corinthians 9:6b says, "He who soweth bountifully shall reap also bountifully." Verse 8 adds, "And God is able to make all grace abound toward you, that ye, always having all sufficiency in all things, may abound to every good work." And there's more: "(Now he that ministereth seed to the sower both minister bread for your food, and multiply your seed sown, and increase the fruits of your righteousness), being enriched in everything to all bountifulness, which causeth through us thanksgiving to God" (vv. 10–11). If you sow bountifully, you will reap bountifully. It's no wonder that our Lord Jesus said, as recorded in Acts 20:35b, "It is more blessed to give than to receive."

These are the principles of giving in the Scripture, and the blessing attendant upon them can be experienced in the life of every faithful steward.

Focusing on the Facts

1. What improper attitudes toward money and giving do some churches exhibit (see pp. 83–84)?

2. Is New Testament giving basically the same as Old Testament giving (see p. 84)?

3. Did Jesus have to pay taxes? Did He pay them (see p. 85)?

4. What question did the Pharisees ask of Jesus, regarding taxes, in an effort to stump Him? What was His answer (see pp. 85–86)?

5. Was the tithe mentioned in the gospels considered freewill giving or required giving (see p. 86)?

6. Since we do not live under the authority of a holy government, is it all right to cheat a little bit when we pay our taxes in order to give more money to God (see pp. 86–87)?

7. As we freely give to God, how will God give back to us (see pp. 87–88)?

8. Why can't we serve God and money (see pp. 88–89)?

9. If we give bountifully we will receive _____ from God (2 Cor. 9:6; see p. 89).

10. Mark 12:41–44, Hebrews 13:16, and Philippians 4:18–19 reveal what important attitude in respect to giving (see pp. 90–91)?

11. Does God want you to get more money so you can give more? Or does He want you to give more of what you have (see p. 91)?

12. Should a person who has continuing debt problems be put in a position of leadership in the church (see p. 92)?

13. Is it mandatory that Christians give ten percent, or can we prayerfully determine that ourselves (see pp. 92–93)?

14. What role should "needs" play in our pattern of giving (see p. 93)?

15. What attitude is God looking for when we give (see p. 94; 2 Cor. 9:7)?

16. Should planning what we give be a part of our giving pattern (see p. 94)?

17. If you have the quality of generosity in your giving, how will God respond (see p. 95)?

Pondering the Principles

1. As Christians we must truly analyze where our treasures are—on earth or in heaven? Think about what you treasure most in this world. Has it been given to God (cf. Matt. 6:19–21)? In fact, if you are having financial difficulties, Matthew 6:19–34 would be a good portion of Scripture to memorize and meditate on.

2. The rich young ruler in Matthew 19:21 discovered that money stood between him and the Lord. Is that possible with you? If your spiritual life is at a low ebb, reread "Does money stand between you and God?" (pp. 89–90), and examine your attitude toward money (cf. 1 Tim. 6:6–11).

3. In Acts 20:35b the Lord Jesus Christ is quoted as saying, "It is more blessed to give than to receive." Is that truth a reality in your life today? Are you hoping to be on the receiving end of a gift, or are you looking for opportunities to give to meet a need? Meditate on our Lord's words and prayerfully consider your own attitude (see p. 95).

Scripture Index